Cambridge Elements

Elements in the Archaeology of Ancient Israel
edited by
Aaron A. Burke
University of California, Los Angeles
Jeremy D. Smoak
University of California, Los Angeles

AGAINST MOAB

Interrogating the Archaeology of Iron Age Jordan

Benjamin W. Porter
University of California, Berkeley

CAMBRIDGE
UNIVERSITY PRESS

Shaftesbury Road, Cambridge CB2 8EA, United Kingdom

One Liberty Plaza, 20th Floor, New York, NY 10006, USA

477 Williamstown Road, Port Melbourne, VIC 3207, Australia

314–321, 3rd Floor, Plot 3, Splendor Forum, Jasola District Centre, New Delhi – 110025, India

103 Penang Road, #05–06/07, Visioncrest Commercial, Singapore 238467

Cambridge University Press is part of Cambridge University Press & Assessment, a department of the University of Cambridge.

We share the University's mission to contribute to society through the pursuit of education, learning and research at the highest international levels of excellence.

www.cambridge.org
Information on this title: www.cambridge.org/9781009547840

DOI: 10.1017/9781009334952

© Benjamin W. Porter 2025

This publication is in copyright. Subject to statutory exception and to the provisions of relevant collective licensing agreements, with the exception of the Creative Commons version the link for which is provided below, no reproduction of any part may take place without the written permission of Cambridge University Press & Assessment.

An online version of this work is published at doi.org/10.1017/9781009334952 under a Creative Commons Open Access license CC-BY-NC 4.0 which permits re-use, distribution and reproduction in any medium for non-commercial purposes providing appropriate credit to the original work is given and any changes made are indicated. To view a copy of this license visit https://creativecommons.org/licenses/by-nc/4.0

When citing this work, please include a reference to the DOI 10.1017/9781009334952

First published 2025

A catalogue record for this publication is available from the British Library

ISBN 978-1-009-54784-0 Hardback
ISBN 978-1-009-33494-5 Paperback
ISSN 2754-3013 (online)
ISSN 2754-3005 (print)

Cambridge University Press & Assessment has no responsibility for the persistence or accuracy of URLs for external or third-party internet websites referred to in this publication and does not guarantee that any content on such websites is, or will remain, accurate or appropriate.

For EU product safety concerns, contact us at Calle de José Abascal, 56, 1°, 28003 Madrid, Spain, or email eugpsr@cambridge.org.

Against Moab

Interrogating the Archaeology of Iron Age Jordan

Elements in the Archaeology of Ancient Israel

DOI: 10.1017/9781009334952
First published online: March 2025

Benjamin W. Porter
University of California, Berkeley

Author for correspondence: Benjamin W. Porter, bwporter@berkeley.edu

Abstract: Known as a place, a people, and a kingdom at various points in the second and first millennia BCE, Moab has long sustained the attention of archaeologists, philologists, and historians, in part because of its adjacent location to ancient Israel. The past 150 years of research in what is today west-central Jordan has proffered a significant corpus of evidence from the region's archaeological sites. However, a critical analysis of this evidence reveals significant gaps in knowledge that challenge attempts to narrate Moab's political, economic, and social history. This Element examines the evidence as well as the debates surrounding Moab's development and decline. This title is also available as open access on Cambridge Core.

Keywords: archaeology, Iron Age, Jordan, Levant, Moab

© Benjamin W. Porter 2025

ISBNs: 9781009547840 (HB), 9781009334945 (PB), 9781009334952 (OC)
ISSNs: 2754-3013 (online), 2754-3005 (print)

Contents

	Introduction	1
1	The Landscape of West-Central Jordan	4
2	Society and Subsistence across the Second Millennium BCE	11
3	Searching for Sihon, Seeking Balak and Eglon	21
4	King Mesha's Vision of Moab	29
5	Locating the Kingdom of Moab	38
6	Beyond the Kemosh Cult	48
7	Responding to Assyrian Imperialism	59
8	The End of Moab?	66
	Conclusion	71
	References	74

Introduction

> Next Chemos, the obscene dread of Moab's sons,
> From Aroar to Nebo, and the wild
> Of Southmost Abarim; in Hesebon
> And Horonaim, Seon's realm, beyond
> The flowery dale of Sibma clad with vines,
> And Eleale to the Asphaltic pool
> Peor his other name, when he enticed
> Israel in Sittim on their march from Nile
> To do him wanton rites, which cost them woe.
> Yet thence his lustful orgies he enlarged
> Even to that hill of scandal, by the grove
> Of Moloch homicide, lust hard by hate;
> Till good Josiah drove them thence to Hell.
> From John Milton's *Paradise Lost*,
> Book One, lines 406–418

Among Moab's many cameo appearances in the centuries following the first millennium BCE is a passing mention in John Milton's *Paradise Lost*, a seventeenth-century epic poem in blank verse recounting Adam and Eve's fall and their expulsion from the Garden of Eden. Moab appears early in the epic's first book (lines 406–418), during a roll call of fallen angels that Satan has assembled in Hell, their new residence. "Chemos" is listed among the angels, noted to be "the obscene dread of Moab's sons." Over the next five lines, Milton traces the territorial realm of this Chemos, listing eight place names (in order): Aroar, Nebo, Abarim, Hesebon, Horonaim, Sibma, Eleale, and the "Asphaltic pool," the Dead Sea. The remaining seven lines describe how Peor, an alternative name for "Chemos," taunted Israel during the Exodus and how he carried out "lustful" orgies on a "hill of scandal."

Knowledgeable readers of the Hebrew Bible have long appreciated Milton's ability to consolidate a range of disparate biblical passages in his epic (Stallard 2011). These exegetical talents are on display in his brief treatment of Moab. Chemos, or Kemosh, appears occasionally in the Bible (1 Kings 11:7) as a "foreign god" and is attributed to Moab as its patron deity (Jeremiah 48:7–13). Place names mentioned in Chemos's territory are largely drawn from later chapters in the Book of Numbers (20–36), where these settlements are the setting for conflicts between Israel, Moab, and the Amorite king Sihon, Milton's "Seon" in line 4. "The flowery dale of Sibmah clad with vines" alludes to prophetic images of spoiled abundance in Isaiah (16: 8–9) and Jeremiah (48:32). The final seven lines gesture to two separate episodes, one in which Israelite men were punished for marrying Moabite women (Numbers 25), and a second in which the Israelite King Solomon constructed (1 Kings 11:7) – and a later Judahite king, Josiah, destroyed (2 Kings 23:13) – a shrine built for Kemosh near Jerusalem.

Milton, of course, was neither a historian, nor a philologist, nor an archaeologist, but a poet. Yet before he is dismissed for the creative licenses he was permitted in biblical exegesis, Milton should be admired for his attempts to do what so many interpreters have done before and after him: Make sense of Moab using fragmentary statements composed and redacted by ancient writers who neither lived in Moab nor were Moabites themselves. After all, Milton's pseudo-historical geography (lines 2–6), in which he plucks the names of towns cited as "Chemos" – affiliated from different biblical passages, is composed using techniques vaguely similar to geographies produced in modern scholarship (e.g., Glueck 1940: 167–181; MacDonald 2000: 171–183). One can only imagine how different *Paradise Lost* might have been if Milton had composed his epic centuries later, following the remarkable archaeological discoveries of the nineteenth and twentieth centuries that shed so much new and complicating light on the biblical world. In the case of Moab, in particular, scholars would like to believe that the past 150 years of archaeological and philological research in the west-central portion of the Hashemite Kingdom of Jordan has significantly advanced our knowledge of the region's Bronze and Iron Age societies. And, to some extent, they are correct. A European missionary's documentation of the Mesha Stele in 1868, a lengthy account of the Moabite king's military campaigns and achievements, was a watershed event in the region's investigation, adding much to the historical record (Dearman 1989). The documentation of archaeological "ruins" by nineteenth-century explorers followed by the more detailed landscape surveys of the twentieth century cataloged an impressive number of settlements available for investigation (e.g., Glueck 1940; Miller 1991; Seetzen 1854). The excavation of Bronze and Iron Age settlements that began in the second half of the twentieth century created a foundation for the investigation of the region's architecture and material culture. The robust debates about the Hebrew Bible's reliability as a historical source have injected much-needed skepticism into research on Jordan's Iron Age societies.

Yet, at the same time, a review of the knowledge that has so far been accumulated about "Moab" is constructed on a shaky scaffolding of fragmentary evidence. The epigraphic evidence – the Mesha Stele inscription, the undecipherable Balu'a stele, and the dozen or so brief and often broken inscriptions found on ceramics and stone objects – raised just as many questions as they offered answers upon their discovery and analysis. The archaeological evidence can be equally beguiling and fragmentary.

Second- and first-millennium BCE[1] settlements in west-central Jordan can be difficult to access, as many were built over in the later Classical and Islamic eras. These later settlements often harvested materials from Bronze and Iron Age buildings when carrying out construction projects, leaving fragmentary in situ evidence to be documented. Some settlements have yet to be excavated; some that have been excavated have been published in ways that make it impossible to answer contemporary research questions on social life or agricultural practices. Many settlements, often ones that are small and difficult to detect in the landscape, are currently at risk of destruction in the wake of much-needed construction that will meet the housing needs of Jordan's growing population.

Of course, one could rightly argue that any investigation of past societies faces similar challenges in the preservation and interpretability of a fragmentary historical record. For Moab, however, the situation is compounded by the unfortunate fact that there are significant gaps in archaeological and epigraphic evidence at key moments in the kingdom's history that make it difficult to trace its political and economic development. Scholars have sought to account for these gaps in evidence in two distinct ways. One way has been to use models drawn from social scientific research. During centuries where evidence is limited or lacking, for instance, these lacunae are attributed to the pastoralist economies of nomadic and semi-nomadic societies that are assumed to have left behind limited amounts of evidence due to low-intensity settlement practices. In turn, the political organization of these "invisible" societies is assumed to be based on extended patrimonial kinship systems, understood as "tribalism" in traditional political anthropological taxonomies (e.g., Fried 1967; Service 1978). While they have proven useful for interpreting archaeological evidence, the models – and the categories on which they rely – have themselves come to stand in for the absent physical evidence, inadvertently creating theoretical "zombies" that are mistaken for historical facts. The second related issue concerns scholars' willingness to overinterpret what is fragmentary and difficult to decipher evidence, whether it is a broken text, a biblical passage whose date of composition is uncertain, or a 50-year-old hand-drawn map of an archaeological site. This lack of source criticism combined with leaps in logic and weak analogical reasoning has crafted "just-so" stories of Moab for audiences that crave letter-perfect

---

[1] Time is denoted here in terms of millennia (e.g., "first millennium BCE") or using the standard metal-age terminology "Iron Age" denoting c. 1200–300 BCE. Because there is no agreement on the chronological division of the Iron Age, nor should space be dedicated to unresolvable debates, the chronological sub-divisions of the Iron Age are set aside here (Iron Age I, Iron Age IIB, etc.) in favor of using centuries (e.g., ninth century).

narratives of ancient Israel's neighbor for their own scholarly and ethno-nationalist projects.

My argument – that current reconstructions of Moab, both as a place and as a historical political entity, rest upon a shaky scaffolding consisting of problematic evidence that is often overinterpreted through anachronistic social scientific models – is an admittedly pessimistic place to begin this extensive treatment. The reader will hopefully forgive my skepticism as we examine the evidence for, and assess the debates concerning, the political, economic, and cultural formations that began in the latter half of the second millennium and extended into the first millennium BCE in west-central Jordan. A rigorous treatment of the evidence, I hope, will not only highlight the discrepancies in current understandings of Moab but will also identify where additional research is needed in the coming decades if we are to grasp, as Milton described, "The obscene dread of Moab's sons."

1 The Landscape of West-Central Jordan

Ancient writers repeatedly placed the toponym and political entity known as "Moab" in what is today a horizontal slice of the longitudinal Transjordan Plateau that runs parallel to the Jordan Rift Valley and today largely coincides with the Madaba and Karak governorates of the Hashemite Kingdom of Jordan (Figure 1; Table 1).[2] West-central Jordan, as this area shall be called here, begins on the eastern side of the Jordan Valley and Dead Sea, and extends approximately 30 km eastward where it gives way to the Arabian Desert. Deep canyons, or *wadis*, segment west-central Jordan into three subregions: the Madaba Plains, the Dhiban Plateau, and the Karak Plateau. Beginning in the southern suburbs of modern 'Amman, the Madaba Plains extends south to the Wadi al-Walla. The Dhiban Plateau rests between the Wadi al-Walla and the Wadi al-Mujib, and the Karak Plateau falls between the Wadi al-Mujib and the Wadi al-Hasa. Four bioclimatic/biogeographic zones are arranged in a series of uneven concentric circles radiating outward from the center of west-central Jordan. A now-degraded patchwork of Mediterranean climatic zones is found in the center, located in the highest altitudes on the western half of the Transjordan Plateau (Figure 2). These zones possess arable Red Mediterranean and Yellow Mediterranean soils and receive sufficient levels of annual precipitation to support rain-fed grain agriculture. Thin Irano-Turanian semi-arid steppe zones border the Mediterranean zone on its east and west sides. Precipitation levels

---

[2] See Ababsa 2014; Bender 1974; Cordova 2007; and Macumber 2008 for in-depth discussions of Jordan's geological and environmental characteristics.

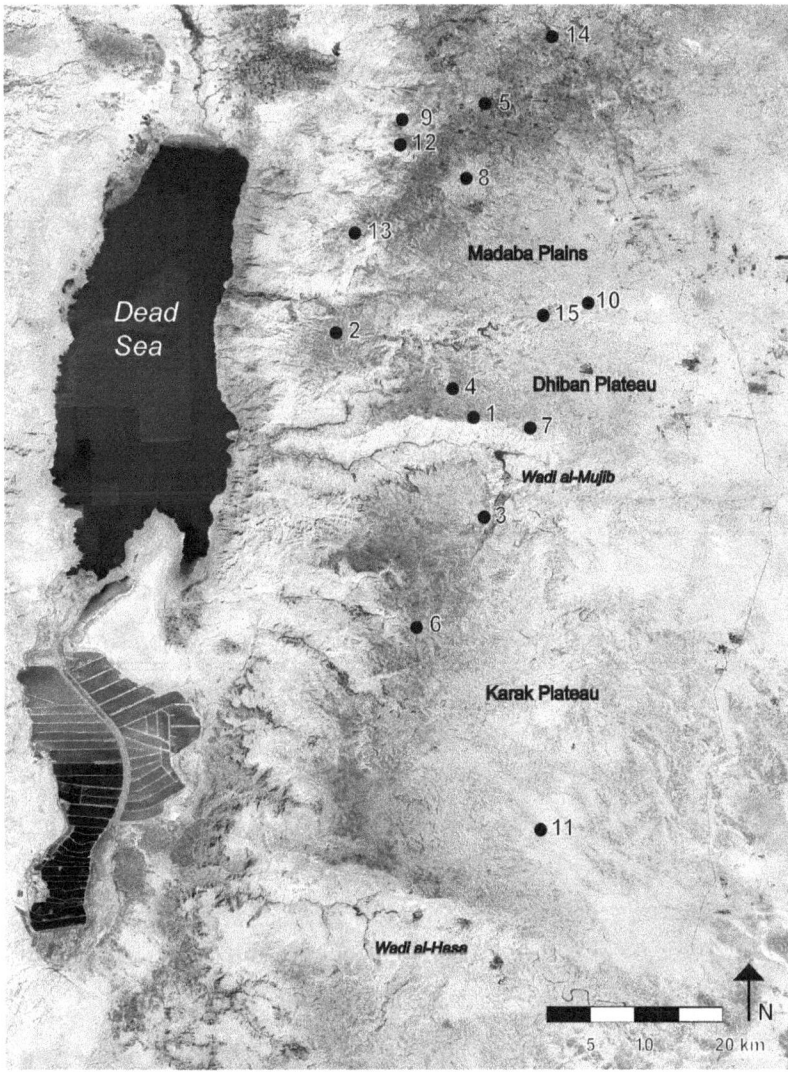

Figure 1 Map of ancient settlements and geographic features in west-central Jordan. Refer to Table 1 for key (Image: B. Porter).

and soil quality are lower here, limiting where, when, and how grain agriculture can be conducted. Further east is the beginning of the Arabian Desert, an arid Sahara-Arabian zone. The region between the eastern shore of the Dead Sea and the Transjordan Plateau in the Jordan Rift Valley is an arid Sudanian Penetration zone that possesses tropical elements. These latter three zones have been and continue to be popular areas for animal grazing, especially during the cooler winter months.

Table 1 List of archaeological site names and their ancient names, when known, in west-central Jordan

No.	Site Name	Ancient Name
1	ʻAroʻer	ʻAroʻer
2	ʻAtaruz	ʻAṭarot
3	Baluʻa	
4	Dhiban	Dibon
5	Hisban	Heshbon
6	Karak	Kir Hareseth (likely)
7	Lahun	
8	Madaba	Madaba
9	al-Mashhad	
10	Mudanya Wadi al-Thamad	Yaḥas (likely)
11	Mudaybiʻ	
12	al-Mukhayyat	Nebo
13	Safra	
14	al-ʻUmayri	
15	WT−13	

Figure 2 The eastern Karak Plateau in summer after the landscape's winter grasses have retreated (Image: Adir Cairn 2; Kh. en-Nsheinish (Miller #353); ©APAAME_20181014_MND-0332. Image: M. Dalton).

Figure 3 The northwest corner of the Karak Plateau in winter, March 2024 (© APAAME_20240304_RHB-0080. Image: R. Bewley).

Precipitation plays an important role in defining these bioclimatic zones. Recordings from weather field stations indicate that west-central Jordan experiences the wet cold winters and hot dry summers that are typical of Mediterranean environments. Precipitation falls mainly between November and April, although amounts vary across the region (el-Naqa 1993) (Figure 3). Precipitation data collected by the Water Authority of Jordan from 1960 until 1990 recorded that the mean annual precipitation of Dhiban was 256.56 mm/yr. At Qatrana, located 40 km to the southeast and on the eastern end of the study area, a dramatically lower average of 90.12 mm was recorded between 1960 and 1989. These amounts are barely sufficient to support rain-fed grain agriculture without substantial investments in infrastructure to store and distribute water. Even brief periods of drought could disrupt agricultural economies, making scarcity a lived reality.

Offering some reprieve from the plateaus' uneven ecology are the wadi canyons that incise the landscape to create drainages that carry fresh water to the Jordan Valley and Dead Sea. Lush riparian zones containing pools of fresh water are found at the bottom of these canyons (Figure 4). Winter precipitation and slow-draining aquifers recharge these pools, providing a source of drinking water for humans and animals even in the hottest months. These riparian habitats support animal life, such as birds, reptiles, crabs, and small mammals.

Figure 4 Riparian zone in summer located at the bottom of the Wadi al-Mujib Canyon. Ponds of freshwater created by precipitation and aquifer drainage exist year-round to support humans, plants, and animals (Image: B. Porter).

Humans did not build large settlements inside these riparian zones, but instead located their populations on nearby ridges so they could access the zones' resources for hunting, gathering, and watering their herds.

The extent to which the Levant, and, specifically, Jordan's environment has changed over the millennia has been the subject of much study (e.g., Cordova 2007; Issar and Zohar 2004; Rosen 2007). The cool, moist, forested, and fluvial landscape in which the earliest hominid populations first subsisted 900,000 years ago began to see aridification c. 12,000 years ago (Cordova 2007: 62–94). Demographic growth and agricultural intensification during the Neolithic Era and Bronze Age instigated landscape degradation that included vegetation removal and soil erosion. These activities, coupled with the gradual warming trends of the Holocene Era, contributed to the largely degraded landscape in which first millennium BCE communities subsisted. Narrowing the resolution to identify changes to the second and first millennium BCE (i.e., the Bronze and Iron Ages), west-central Jordan is frustrated by the lack of environmental proxy evidence in the immediate area (Porter 2014). Proxies documented in adjacent regions, such as the Dead Sea, must therefore be used to extrapolate environmental changes. To summarize a wide array of evidence for the sake of expediency, climatic conditions during the first millennium BCE in west-central Jordan was similar to today, with cool wet winters and warm dry summers.

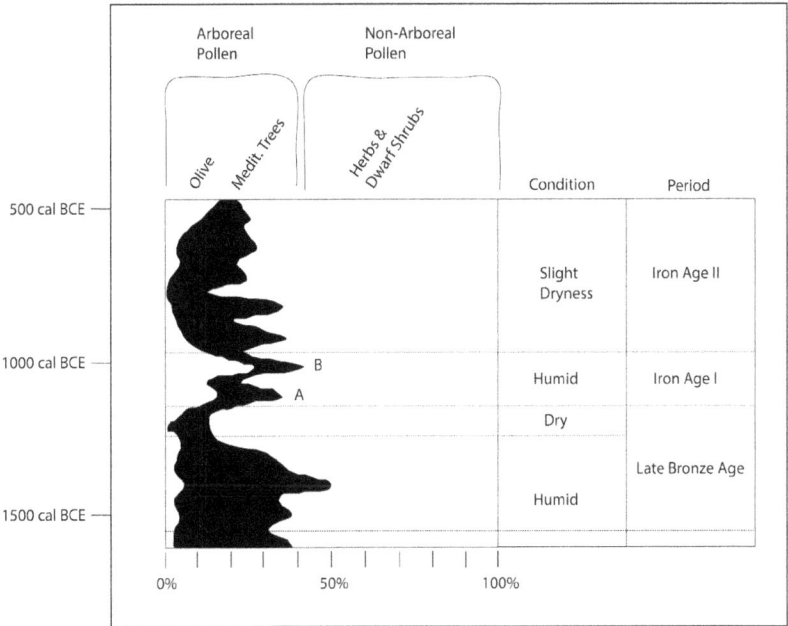

Figure 5 A pollen core from Lake Kinneret reveals changes in climatic conditions during the late second and first millennium BCE. (A) and (B) indicate periods of relative cool temperatures and wetter conditions at the end of the second millennium BCE (Image: B. Porter; data adapted from Langgut, Finkelstein, and Litt 2013).

However, extended periods of wetter years and drier years did occur (Figure 5). The unreliability of winter precipitation impacted the second- and first-millennium societies of west-central Jordan, requiring them to organize their subsistence economies to sustain them during periods of scarcity (Porter 2013).

Despite the region's dynamic topography and precarious conditions, west-central Jordan's populations were connected to their Levantine neighbors and, indeed, Mesopotamia, Arabia, and the Mediterranean Basin by a network of roads. At least three longitudinal roads run through west-central Jordan. One road passed along the eastern shore of the Dead Sea and continued north through the Jordan Valley. A second road, the so-called King's Highway, extended from Aqaba or Ma'an to northern destinations such as Damascus and Aleppo. In west-central Jordan, this road passed through the region's major settlements such as Karak and Madaba. Smaller roads connected towns to this main artery through which goods and peoples flowed. A third largely longitudinal road ran along the eastern fringe of the Karak Plateau, skirting the eastern tributaries of the Wadi al-Mujib before passing through Mudayna Wadi al-Thamad[3] on its way to northern destinations (Dolan and Edwards 2020). Multiple east–west running roads connected settlements with each other. One prominent road began at Rabba in the center of the Karak Plateau and ran west to Karak before descending to the Dead Sea. Another important road ran northwest to southeast through the Fajj al-'Usaiker that connects the Arabian Desert with Karak.

The region's environmental conditions therefore presented west-central Jordan's communities with a viable yet challenging setting with which to organize their livelihoods. On the one hand, select Mediterranean zones offered sufficient conditions to sustain sedentary settlements through agro-pastoralism. Yet, on the other hand, the arid and semi-arid zones that encircled these more viable zones either limited or prevented permanent settlements. All the while, this patchwork landscape was connected to each other through roads, large and small, a fact that never isolated west-central Jordan from its neighbors in any direction. A sensitivity to these local ecological circumstances helps refine a long-standing "desert and sown" paradigm that informs popular and scholarly understandings of Jordan's extensive culture history (e.g., Bell 1908; LaBianca 1990, to name only a few). Such models emphasize periodic episodes of settlement intensification in which mobile communities gradually adopted sedentary lifestyles, founding new settlements and rehabilitating former ones. These commitments to sedentary life were often followed by investments in infrastructure that increased food production for the sake of sustaining larger populations and participating in regional markets. When political, economic, or environmental circumstances no longer encouraged sedentary lifestyles, they were exchanged, sometimes gradually, for mobile ones in which pastoralism dictated the movement of communities between summer and winter pastures.

The application of desert and sown models to Jordan's culture history have often understood sedentary and mobile lifestyles as stark either/or choices available to communities, a decision that portrays Jordan's history as an oscillating political economic system shifting between prosperous "booms" in sedentary lifeways followed by disastrous "busts" in which households have no choice but to turn to mobile practices to sustain themselves. The available archaeological and textual evidence indicates that households responded in different and unpredictable ways from each other, a suggestion that macro-economic subsistence models do not necessarily offer sufficiently granular resolutions for historical analysis. For the second- and first-millennium BCE

---

[3] The archaeological site known by variations of "Khirbat al-Mudayna on the Wadi ath-Thamad," what is likely ancient Yaḥaz, is abbreviated here as "Mudayna Wadi al-Thamad."

west-central Jordan, specifically, the evidence for sedentary life can sometimes be difficult to detect and interpret, leading some analysts to downplay its importance, as we shall see next.

2 Society and Subsistence across the Second Millennium BCE

The search for Moab's origins have traditionally begun in the second millennium BCE when a confluence of Egyptian and biblical sources first placed the toponym east of the Dead Sea. While the Egyptian sources are rather fragmentary, as will soon be clear, the Hebrew Bible describes Moab in much greater detail as politically organized enough to be portrayed as a kingdom. These textual representations of Moab have led scholars to search the archaeological record of second-millennium west-central Jordan for evidence of a regional political polity, with, as shall be argued here, little success. Instead, what has so far been discovered and studied reveals a dynamic landscape of modestly sized sedentary and mobile societies that organized their political goals and economic practices at local levels. This understanding of second-millennium west-central Jordan must be considered when evaluating the biblical sources, a concern that will be taken up soon following the presentation of west-central Jordan's archaeological evidence.

Following a nearly sixteen-century period of sedentary settlement intensification during the Levantine Early Bronze Age (Philip 2008; Richard 2014), west-central Jordan experienced a notable decline in political and economic development during the second millennium BCE. Surveys across the region have recovered artifacts from the surfaces of archaeological sites that can be assigned relative dates to the Middle Bronze (c. 2000–1500 BCE) and Late Bronze (c. 1500–1200 BCE) Ages. In the Madaba Plains, Middle and Late Bronze Age ceramic vessels were documented in multi-period settlements in limited amounts compared to earlier (i.e., the Early Bronze Age) and later (i.e., the first millennium BCE Iron Age) eras (Ibach 1987: 155–158; figs. 3.2–3.3). Excavations at settlements in the Madaba Plains, such as Hisban, al-'Umayri, Iktanu, and Jalul identified evidence for Bronze Age sedentary settlements (Clark et al. 2015). At al-'Umayri, the best preserved and documented Bronze Age settlement on the Madaba Plains, a ~1.5 ha settlement was encircled by fortifications constructed in the seventeenth century (strata 16–15) (Herr, Clark, and Bramlett 2009). After a two-century hiatus between c. 1550 and 1350 BCE, the settlement was reoccupied and a monumental building, either a palace or a temple, was constructed and used until the mid-twelfth century (strata 14–12). South of the Madaba Plains, archaeological surveys on the Dhiban and Karak Plateaus have documented a similar limited settlement pattern using second-millennium ceramic vessels found on the surfaces of ancient sites (Clark, Koucky, and Parker 2006: 38; Ji and Lee 2000: Table 4; Miller 1991: 308–309).[4] Bronze Age material culture has also been documented in later Iron Age contexts, attesting to the presence of second-millennium settlement activity that later building projects obscured. So while there is currently a frustrating scarcity of stratified evidence with which to characterize mid-second-millennium west-central Jordan on the Dhiban and Karak Plateaus, there are tantalizing clues that more evidence could be discovered in the future.

One explanation for why there is a limited amount of evidence for settlement activity is that sedentary life was likely confined to small towns and encampments that were occupied for short durations of time, a condition that Egyptian textual sources support. Between the sixteenth and twelfth centuries BCE, the Egyptian New Kingdom's Eighteenth, Nineteenth, and Twentieth Dynasty pharaohs controlled much of the southern Levant, including the Jordan Valley (Mumford 2013). Although the Bronze Age settlements of northwest Jordan and the Jordan Valley may have been under Egypt's sway, regions further to the south likely sat just beyond Egypt's control. Egyptian scribes described the region, often in disparaging terms, as the domain of the *shasu* or, in Amarna Akkadian, *sutu* or *shutu* (Kitchen 1992; Redford 1982).[5] These groups were characterized as mobile or semi-mobile groups that occasionally raided Canaanite towns and Egyptian garrisons. While *shasu* are described as living mobile lifestyles in some sources, other sources describe groups living in settlements. What was likely an itinerary of a military campaign during the reign of the Eighteenth Dynasty pharaoh Thutmose III lists four towns – *tipun*, *'ubir*, *yarutu*, and *harkur* – in western Jordan (Redford 1982). The first listed settlement may be Dhiban and the final town, Karak; the middle two names are difficult to assign with any certainty. If there were fifteenth-century settlements at Dhiban and Karak to be attacked, stratified archaeological evidence for both towns have so far not been documented.[6] In a later text located on the wall of Ramesses II's temple at Luxor, a town (*dmi*) in the "land of Moab" named *b[w] trt*, possibly modern Rabba, is mentioned in a campaign itinerary that is often

---

[4] On the Karak Plateau, Miller reported fifteen Middle Bronze Age sites and twenty-nine Late Bronze Age sites where at least five ceramic sherds from each period were discovered during pedestrian survey (Miller 1991: 308–309; cf. Routledge 2004: 78–82). Ji and Lee report that no evidence for Middle Bronze Age settlement was found in their survey of the Dhiban Plateau and only ten of the 421 surveyed settlements had limited evidence for Late Bronze Age settlement (Ji and Lee 2000: 504). Similarly, Clark, Cocky, and Parker report next to no Middle Bronze Age evidence and slightly more Late Bronze Age evidence on the eastern Karak Plateau (Clark, Cocky, and Parker 2006: 38).

[5] See Kitchen 1992; Redford 1982; and Timm 1989: 5–60 for a complete treatment of Egyptian sources on second millennium BCE Jordan.

[6] However, ceramic vessels identified in surveys and later deposits attest to the presence of human activities at both sites during this time (e.g., Routledge 2004: Fig. 8.5; Miller 1991: 89) although it is impossible to characterize these activities from the evidence.

dated to the ninth year of Ramesses II's rule, c. 1270 BCE (Kyle 1908).[7] This nod to a "land of Moab" in this passage is so far the earliest known mention of the region in historical records. Although the written sources present two different depictions of the region's settlement organization, one can certainly imagine an arrangement in which sedentary and mobile populations resided next to each other during this time.

The political and economic organization of west-central Jordan becomes somewhat clearer during the closing centuries of the second millennium BCE, a period of upheaval throughout the Eastern Mediterranean (Cline 2014). Egypt's power over the Canaanite city-states waned during the twelfth century, leaving local elites once again in charge of the Eastern Mediterranean littoral. If west-central Jordan saw any disruption from Egypt's withdrawal or the broader Eastern Mediterranean decline, it is difficult to discern any such patterns in the available evidence. Instead, there are signs of continuity during the transition from the Bronze to the Iron Age, that is, between the late-thirteenth and mid-tenth centuries BCE. Most archaeological surveys across west-central Jordan report a noticeable increase in the number of documented late-second-millennium settlements. A landscape survey on the Madaba Plains identified thirty sites in a 10-km radius around Hisban (Ibach 1987: 160–163; table 3.8; fig. 3.5), while 19 out of 421 identified sites on the Dhiban Plateau dated to the twelfth and eleventh centuries (Ji and Lee 1998: Table 1). Miller's survey of the Karak Plateau identified seventy-two sites across 875 km^2, twenty-five of which yielded more than five Iron Age ceramic sherds (Miller 1991: 309). Survey on the Karak Plateau's eastern desert fringe identified seventy-one sites that ranged from single-building farms and defensive towers to small settlements (Clark, Koucky, and Parker 2006: 38–42; figs. 2.1–2.2).[8]

These surveys indicate that there was a widespread tendency throughout west-central Jordan to found small settlements.[9] However, those settlements that were established along the edges of the Wadi al-Mujib and its tributaries are the region's

---

[7] The interpretation and dating of the Luxor texts are debated (Darnell and Jasnow 1993).

[8] These survey projects were largely conducted between 1970 and 2000, and used vehicular rather than pedestrian survey methods. The random field walking of transects to identify sherd scatters, for instance, was not performed on a regular basis. Also, investigations did not include the sides and bottoms of wadi canyons. The population of west-central Jordan has grown considerably in the last few decades with commensurate building activities, so many of these ephemeral sites are likely no longer available for investigation.

[9] Excavations and surveys have recently detected a handful of late second-millennium settlements on the western edge of the Madaba Plains near the Wadi Zarqa-Maʻin, including Boz al-Mushelle (Routlede and Halbertsma forthcoming), ʻAyun al-Dhib (Danielson et al. 2024), and Khirbat Safra (Gregor 2021; Gregor et al. 2021). At Safra, recent on-going excavations have identified a 1.0 ha agricultural settlement 17 km southwest of Madaba. A casemate wall fortification system

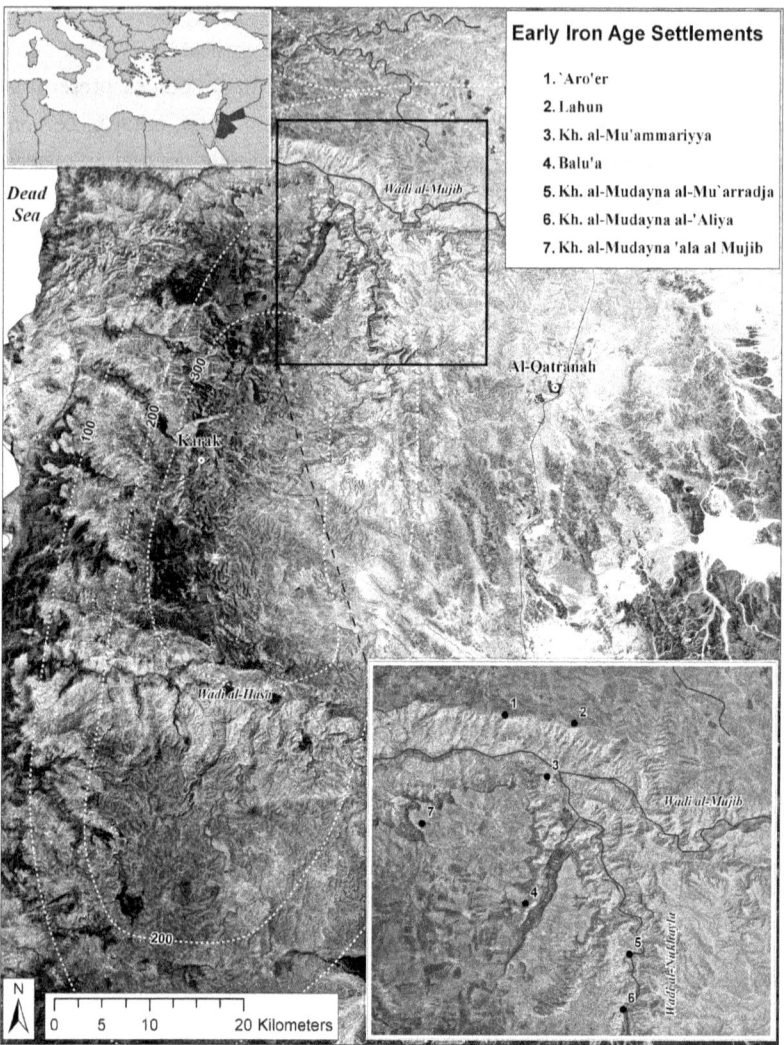

Figure 6 Map of the Karak Plateau detailing the late second-millennium BCE settlements in the Wadi al-Mujib corridor (Image: B. Porter).

best documented (Figure 6). Seven settlements have been excavated to various degrees, including, from north to south, 'Aro'er, Lahun, Khirbat al-Mu'ammariyya, Balu'a, Khirbat al-Mudayna al-Mu'arradja, Khirbat al-Mudayna al-'Aliya, and Khirbat al-Mudayna al-Mujib (Porter 2013). For those settlements whose

---

surrounds multiple domestic residences that were destroyed in the tenth century BCE. Soon after this destruction event, a less-substantial settlement was founded again and lasted into the eighth century BCE. Excavations have only recently begun at Safra, so this interpretation should be considered preliminary.

perimeters can be discerned, their overall size ranged between 1.0 (al-Mudayna al-Mu'arradjeh) and 2.2 (al-Mudayna al-'Aliya) ha (Routledge 2004: Table 5.2).[10] These settlements were spaced between 5 and 6 km apart from each other with no evidence for farmsteads between them. These settlements shared a similar design in which a series of residences were arranged in an oval pattern with their entrances facing into large plazas. The rear walls of these residences doubled as part of the settlement's perimeter wall. Towers and small gates strengthened this fortification system at al-Mudayna al-'Aliya, al-Mu'ammariyya, al-Mudayna al-Mu'arradja, and Lahun.

Residencies were built from local stone and were designed using variations on the Iron Age pillared buildings that have been documented throughout the southern Levant, particularly in the Central Highlands north and south of Jerusalem (Faust and Bunimovitz 2003; Shiloh 1970). Each building was designed to provide shelter for a family and consisted of multiple small rooms used for storage, food production and consumption, craft production, and other subsistence duties. At al-Mudayna al-'Aliya, residences were notably different in size, a sign that some households possessed more wealth and capacity for subsistence than their neighbors (Figure 7). Excavations determined that some residences fell out of use before al-Mudayna al-'Aliya was abandoned and were used as trash middens for neighboring buildings. Other buildings showed signs that they were abruptly abandoned. For instance, in Building 500, well-protected storage bins in an attached granary were left filled with grain intended for baking in a nearby kitchen (Farahani et al. 2016: Fig. 2.7).

While the political and ethnic identities of the al-Mujib settlements are debated (and will be discussed in Section 3), their subsistence economics, largely based on animal husbandry and grain agriculture, have been reconstructed in detail. The analysis of zooarchaeological evidence from al-Mudayna al-'Aliya identified an unsurprising dependence on domesticated sheep and goat, and to a lesser extent on cattle and pig (Lev-Tov, Porter, and Routledge 2011) (Table 2). A companion archaeobotanical investigation of carbonized plant remains provides additional information about the diets of humans and animals in the settlement (Table 3) (Farahani et al. 2016). Domesticated barley (*Hordeum* sp.) overwhelmingly dominated the assemblage with only trace amounts of wheat (*Tritium* sp.), no doubt due to the settlement's location in a semi-arid zone where barley can better withstand reduced moisture levels (Farahani et al. 2016: Table 2.3). Other common domesticates, in order of

---

[10] Later construction episodes make it impossible to determine the size of 'Aro'er and Balu'a in the late second millennium BCE.

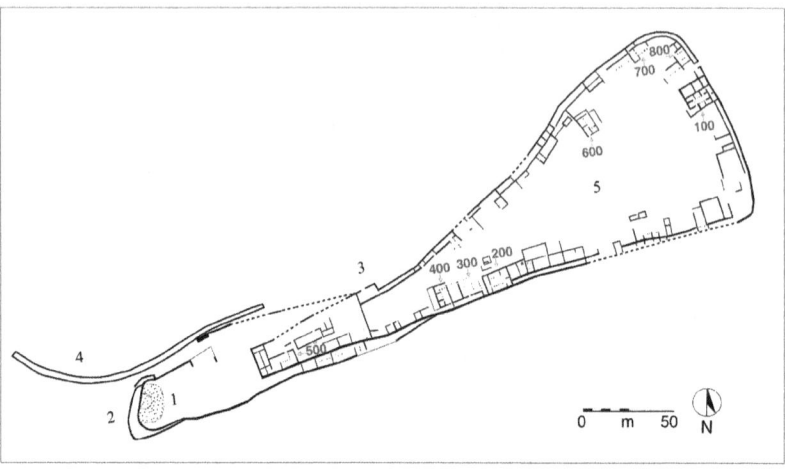

Figure 7 (A) Map of Mudayna al-'Aliya denoting Buildings 100 through 800, tower (1), moat (2), a possible gated entrance (3), paved pathway (4), and plaza (5). (B) Aerial image of Mudayna al-'Aliya looking to the north (Image: Kh. Mdeinet Aliya (Miller, no. 143) ©APAAME_20011005_DLK-0021. Image: D. L. Kennedy).

abundance, were fig (*Ficus carica*), grape (*Vitis vinifera*), lentil, millet, and legume. Archaeobotanical samples collected from stone-lined bins located inside two buildings reveal that these plant materials provided food for both

Table 2 List of faunal evidence documented at Khirbat al-Mudayna al-'Aliya

Scientific Name	Common Name	NISP	Percent	MNI
Ardeidae/Ciconiidae	Heron or stork	1	+	1
Aves	Unidentifiable birds	10	2	–
Bos taurus	Domestic cattle	11	3	1
Camelus sp.	Camel	1	+	1
Canis familiaris	Domestic dog	3	1	2
Capra hircus	Domestic goat	10	2	3
Cervus elaphus	Red deer	1	+	1
Equus asinus	Ass or onager	8	2	1
Equus caballus	Horse	12	3	2
Equus sp.	Horse, ass, or onager	16	4	3
cf. Erinaceidae	Possible hedgehog	1	+	1
Osteichthyes	Bony fish	1	+	1
Ovis aries	Domestic sheep	8	2	2
Ovis/Capra	Sheep or goat	229	53	7
Passeriformes	Perching bird	1	+	1
Potamon potamios	Freshwater crab	100	23	27
Rodentia	Rodent	12	3	2
Sus scrofa	Pig	6	1	1
Unidentifiable bones		1798	–	–
Total identifiable		431		29
Grand total		2229		

+ amount fell below 1 percent
NISP = Number of identified species
MNI = Minimum number of individuals

humans and animals. Bins in one building (Building 100) contained less processed plant materials in which barley was mixed with weedy taxa, while bins in another building (Building 500) contained more processed grains. The cleaner bins in the latter context were reserved for bread production in the nearby kitchen, while those in the former context were likely held in reserve for animal fodder during the late summer and early fall months when field stubble had been completely grazed (Farahani et al. 2016: 46–54).

Wild animals supplemented but did not dominate this subsistence economy. Zooarchaeological analysis of the al-Mudayna al-'Aliya evidence identified birds, fish, and deer that were hunted or fished in the region's vicinity. Notable was the consumption of large numbers of semi-terrestrial freshwater crabs (*Potamon potamios*) whose habitat is located in and around the freshwater pools in the wadi bottoms. Oxygen and carbon isotopes from these ancient crab

Table 3 Absolute counts of major domesticate seeds across eighty-five analysed samples

Common Name	Scientific Name	Count	% of Total
Domesticated barley (subspecies indeterminate)	*Hordeum vulgare*	4,068	66.10%
Two-row domesticated barley	*Hordeum vulgare* subsp. *distichum*	1,021	17%
Fig	*Ficus carica*	750	12.20%
Grape (seed)	*Vitis vinifera*	120	2%
Indeterminate Cereal		90	1.50%
Six-row domesticated barley	*Hordeum vulgare* subsp. *vulgare*	54	<1%
Lentil	*Lens culinaris*	14	<1%
Large legume	*Fabaceae*	10	<1%
Common millet	*Panicum miliaceum*	7	<1%
Wheat (species indeterminate)	*Triticum* sp.	6	<1%
Grape (raisin)	*Vitis vinifera*	4	<1%
Bitter vetch	*Vicia ervilia*	4	<1%
Free threshing wheat	*Triticum aestivum/durum*	1	<1%
Emmer wheat	*Triticum dicoccum*	1	<1%
Total		**6,150**	

remains were examined alongside modern crab specimens and the pools in which they were sampled (Farahani et al. 2023). A high correlation in oxygen isotope values between modern crab carapaces and the water in the specific pools where they were sampled suggests that the variability in isotopic values of ancient crab specimens reflects an opportunistic harvesting practice. That is, humans were moving from pool to pool, gathering crabs as they encountered them rather than engaging in intentional aquaculture in which crabs were raised and harvested in specific pools.

Weedy and wild plant taxa found in al-Mudayna al-'Aliya's archaeobotanical assemblage indicate that humans used the al-Mujib's riparian zone in their subsistence economies despite the arduous trip from their settlements. Taxa with higher water requirements such as plantain (*Plantago* sp.), fumewort (*Fumaria* sp.), and sedges (*Cyperaceae*) entered al-Mudayna al-'Aliya either through the cropping of domesticated plants in which these weedy taxa were commingled or through their consumption by domesticated animals whose dung humans gathered for fuel in their settlements (Farahani et al. 2016: 43).

The al-Mujib settlements were growing and gathering plants, grazing herds, and hunting wild animals in these riparian zones.

Like their plant and animal economies, the craft economies of the al-Mujib settlements supported the immediate needs of members. Vessels made from organic materials such as baskets were likely the most commonly used containers; these are impossible to detect today due to preservation issues. The settlements also carried out low-intensity ceramic vessel manufacturing using raw materials found in their immediate vicinity (Porter 2007; Routledge et al. 2014). Bowls, kraters, storage jars, and cooking pots were dominant forms (Steiner 2013; Swinnen 2009: fig. 21; Worschech 2014: 168–173, among others). Some vessels are similar in form and design to those found in the Central Highlands north and south of Jerusalem during the twelfth and eleventh centuries.[11] Most vessels went undecorated save an occasional exterior white slip. An exception was a collection of open vessels, bowls and kraters, with vertical wavy lines descending from their rims that were painted with red pigment whose recipes were high in iron and magnesium oxides (Porter and Speakman 2008) (Figure 8). These crudely decorated bowls have been identified in multiple al-Mujib settlements, including Balu'a (Worschech 2014: 169–171) and Mudayna al-'Aliya (Routledge et al. 2014: Fig. 4: 5, 11, 15).[12] These design elements may have been added to these vessels to simulate the spillage of their contents, a signal of abundance in a resource-scarce environment where food was a form of wealth and the sharing of food was a strategy in building and sustaining community (Porter 2013: 120–127).

Early Iron Age settlements on the Wadi al-Mujib and its tributaries show a clear preference for nucleation, strongly fortifiable locations, generous settlement spacing, and proximity to the diverse resources of the riparian zones in wadi bottoms. Despite these shared preferences, the al-Mujib communities were not occupied at the same time.[13] Rather, absolute and relative dates of occupation and abandonment from the eight known settlements in the al-Mujib corridor reveals that settlement practices were highly unstable and commitment to sedentary life persisted for only a few generations before settlements were gradually abandoned. Disaffected households peeled off from settlements to travel up the wadi corridor to found new settlements, a process described as extensification (Porter et al. 2014). It is difficult to determine what factors perpetuated this pattern. That households were shifting frequently between

---

[11] See Routledge 2000: 43–47 and Porter 2007: 241–252 for a discussion of ceramic vessel comparanda.

[12] See Porter 2013: 166, note 17 for a list of additional pieces of evidence.

[13] Despite this author and his colleagues repeatedly demonstrating how the al-Mujib communities were not occupied at the same time (e.g., Porter et al. 2014), scholars seeking to prove the existence of a late-second millennium early kingdom of Moab conveniently ignore this point (Finkelstein and Lipschits 2011; Luria 2021).

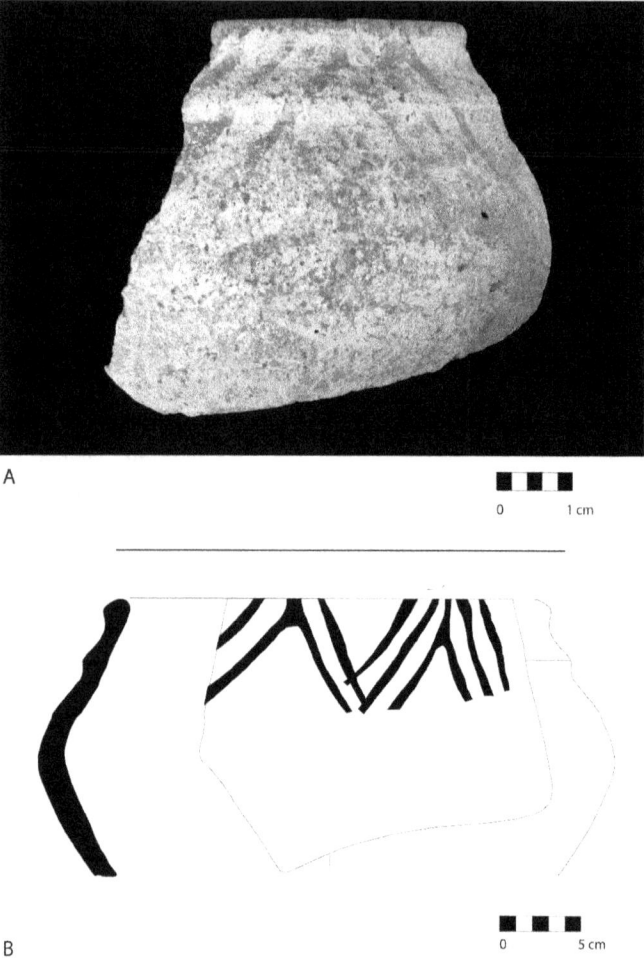

Figure 8 A rim fragment (A) and a profile drawing (B) of two different red-dripped ceramic vessels (Image: B. Porter).

sedentary and nomadic, or at least semi-nomadic, lifestyles, neither explains the "messiness" of the evidence nor does it explain what was pushing and pulling households to make these subsistence decisions. One is tempted to cite changing climate conditions as a "push" factor, yet the limited amount of proxy evidence available that was presented earlier does not point to major changes. Nor does west-central Jordan's location on the eastern fringes of New Kingdom Egypt's control of the southern Levant offer a satisfying push explanation for these patterns. The currently available evidence suggests that settlements were "pulled" into unoccupied frontier zones that offered distinct and circumscribed resources in and adjacent to wadi riparian zones.

3 Searching for Sihon, Seeking Balak and Eglon

What is notable about the archaeological evidence for west-central Jordan's late second-millennium societies is how it disappoints attempts to confirm the Hebrew Bible's description of the region's political organization in the twelfth and eleventh centuries. Multiple biblical passages describe ancient Israel's encounters with west-central Jordan's inhabitants upon their arrival in the Levant (e.g., Numbers 21–25; Deuteronomy 2; among others). Numbers 21:13 demarcates the Arnon River, the modern Wadi al-Mujib, as a territorial border between what the biblical text presents as two fully formed political polities. The Hebrew Bible reports that prior to Israel's arrival, an Amorite kingdom under the leadership of the king Sihon won the *mišor*, as the region north of the Arnon was coined (i.e., the Madaba Plains and the Dhiban Plateau) from the Moabites. This earlier conflict was memorialized in a brief poem in Numbers 21: 27–30 known as the Song of Heshbon, named for Sihon's capital, modern Hisban. Following this war, Moab's territory was reportedly confined south of the Arnon (i.e., the Karak Plateau). Enter the Israelites who requested safe passage through the *mišor* from Sihon in order to reach Canaan west of the Jordan River, a request the Amorite king denied, leading to a battle in which Israel conquered the Amorites.[14] Sensing a threat on his northern border, Balak, Moab's king, asked a local diviner, Balaam, to curse Israel, an act that would hopefully weaken or repel the new arrivals (Numbers 22–24). Under the Israelite god Yahweh's sway, Balaam defied Balak's request and instead issued four oracles in which Balaam blessed Israel and offered prophecies of their success during the next few centuries. Despite Balaam's treasonous act, no physical conflicts between Israel and Moab are described at this time and readers are led to presume that the former left the latter's territory intact. Israel's leader Moses is reported to have executed Israelite men who intermingled with Moabite and Midianite women, relationships that led the men to worship foreign gods such as Baal of Peor (Numbers 25:1–5). Before Moses died at Mount Nebo, he divided the defeated Sihon's territory, along with that of a neighboring king, Og of Bashan, between three Israelite tribes, Reuben, Gad, and half of Manasseh, who valued the territory for its pasture land (Numbers 32:34). Reuben received the northern portion of the *mišor*, including the towns of Nebo and Heshbon, while Gad received the southern half that included ʻAṭarot and Dibon, both located on the Dhiban Plateau. After settling in Canaan, the Israelites occasionally interacted with Moab. Judges 3, for instance,

---

[14] This war is recounted in Deuteronomy 2:26–35 and in Joshua 12: 2–5, although the latter with slightly different geographic parameters. Another battle between the two groups is reported in Judges 11:19–28.

notes that the Moabite king Eglon ruled over Israel for eighteen years until the Israelite judge Ehud assassinated him.

Early twentieth-century interpreters of the Numbers narrative considered the account to be a reliable oral tradition passed down through time until it was enshrined in the written biblical text (e.g., Bright 1959: 128–129; 141–142).[15] Using biblical archaeological techniques, scholars anticipated that material evidence for politically organized second-millennium Amorite and Moabite kingdoms would be identifiable in west-central Jordan. A second and distinct settlement pattern north of the Wadi al-Mujib would hypothetically follow just prior to or during the twelfth century that could be culturally affiliated to the Israelites. Such expectations are on display in Nelson Glueck's sweeping synthesis of Jordan's cultural history based on his extensive archaeological surveys between 1932 and 1947 (Glueck 1939, 1940). Glueck used artifacts, namely ceramic vessels, that he collected from surfaces to date sites' settlement histories. Glueck also used historical geography to identify the names of ancient settlements using either their geographic position relative to better-known settlements, or historical toponymy to identify the names of ancient settlements in their modern names (e.g., ancient Heshbon and modern Hisban). Among other achievements, Glueck used his survey evidence and an uncritical reading of the biblical sources to pace out the territorial borders of Jordan's Iron Age kingdoms, taking special interest in archaeological sites and natural features north of the Wadi al-Mujib to define Sihon's territory (Glueck 1939: 242–251, 1940: 171–173). Glueck assumed that the stone-built towers he observed on the eastern half of the Madaba Plains and Dhiban Plateau were constructed by Sihon to defend his territory. Later research on these settlements and landscape features, however, determined that they were founded in the mid first millennium and served as agricultural farmsteads; these structures were expanded later in time when the Roman army rehabilitated them for their military defense network, the Limes Arabicus (Clark, Koucky, and Parker 2006: 38–42). Archaeologists followed up Glueck's inquiry with research at Hisban where evidence for Sihon's capital could hopefully be identified. Excavations determined, however, that the settlement's Bronze Age and much of its Iron Age settlement was dismantled during the construction of later Classical and Islamic Era buildings. Large numbers of diagnostic ceramic vessels found in dumps and poorly stratified phases (Stratum 21–19) above the bedrock attested to the presence of a late second-millennium settlement (Ray 2001: 75–116). This poor preservation prevents any characterization of Hisban's settlement in light

---

[15] Bright concludes his discussion about the complexities of the narrative with, "Though we cannot reconstruct the events in detail, *we may be sure* that the tradition rests upon the memory of historical events" (1959: 129; italics added for emphasis).

of the events described in the Numbers account nor can the settlement's political and economic role in the region be determined.[16]

Biblical scholarship and archaeological research have advanced considerably since Glueck's synthesis and early research at Hisban. Much debate has focused on the content and composition date of Numbers 21: 27–30, the "Song of Heshbon," a poetic account of the battle between the Amorites and the Moabites, and the former's reported conquest of the *mišor* (Milgrom 1990: 462–463). Because the poem describes an event prior to ancient Israel's arrival in Jordan and is laudatory of the victorious Amorites (i.e., Israel's adversary), commentators have suggested that an Amorite poet may have composed the song that was preserved in oral traditions until it was set down later in the biblical text. One possible reason for embedding a presumed "archaic" non-Israelite source in Numbers was that it certified for audiences that the Moabites had lost the *mišor* before Israel's arrival, and, therefore, Israel had followed Yahweh's decree that they not violate Moab's territory (Deuteronomy 2:19). The Song contains detailed information about the *mišor's* settlements, suggesting that its author had first-hand knowledge of the region. Petter's treatment is the most recent and comprehensive attempt to date the Song close in time to the events it describes. While acknowledging that the Song lacks archaic linguistic elements one might expect from an early source, he argues that an early date "is the most simple and effective explanation for the presence" of the song's peculiar syntactical and thematic features (Petter 2014: 54). In fact, for Petter, many passages in Numbers 21–25 preserves memories of late second-millennium conflicts between tribes – Reuben, Gad, Amorite, and Moabite – in west-central Jordan that were written down at a later point during the text's composition. However, he wisely points out that the archaeological evidence at settlements in the *mišor* (e.g., Hisban, Madaba, and al-'Umayri) is too ambiguous to assign to a specific ethnic group (2014: 98).

While scholars are not wrong to suspect that Numbers 21–25 may document the political and cultural milieu of late second-millennium west-central Jordan, there are multiple reasons why these passages were likely composed at a later date. One common argument is that the text was written during or after the early ninth century BCE to celebrate the kingdom of Israel's territorial expansion into the *mišor* under the Omride Dynasty.[17] As will be discussed in Section 4 in more

---

[16] Notably, excavations at al-'Umayri, a settlement 11 km north of Hisban, identified a Bronze Age settlement that was intermittently occupied throughout the second millennium (Herr, Clark, and Bramlett 2009). There is so far no evidence indicating that al-'Umayri, whose ancient name is unknown, was Sihon's capital.

[17] There is no space here to describe arguments that the Song is a work of Israelite cultural memory. The frequent appearances that Sihon and Heshbon make in the Hebrew Bible signified Israel's

detail, the Mesha Inscription (MI hereafter), a ninth-century text commemorating the Moabite king Mesha's achievements, describes how the kingdom of Israel controlled two regions in the *mišor*, the "Land of Madaba " and the "Land of 'Aṭarot." Mesha reports that he took captive the "Men of Gad," presumably members of the Israelite tribe of Gad, in addition to "Men of Sharon" and "Men of Maḥarot" in 'Aṭarot. According to this extra-biblical source, then, communities aligned with the kingdom of Israel were living north of the Wadi al-Mujib during the early ninth century. The outstanding question is when, exactly, these groups came to settle in the region. As has been demonstrated so far, while archaeological evidence confirms that small villages were littered across the region during the late second millennium, the material evidence is silent on the cultural identities of the people who lived in them.

Ambiguities also persist when searching for clues to early Moab in the evidence documented south of the Wadi al-Mujib. As already noted, the Numbers (e.g., Numbers 21:13) and Judges narratives limit Moab's territory to the Karak Plateau. These and adjacent passages describe Moab's political organization as a kingdom governed by royal leaders who could muster armies in defense of their territory. Three kings are mentioned: an anonymous king who battled Sihon (Number 21:26); Balak, who commissioned Balaam to curse the Israelites (Numbers 22–24); and Eglon, who defeated Israel and ruled over them for eighteen years until the Israelite assassin Ehud murdered him in his palace (Judges 3:12–30). Early historians of Moab had little reason to doubt the Bible's characterization of Moab's political organization.[18] Glueck likewise used the text when synthesizing the evidence he collected in his survey (Glueck 1939: 121–122; cf. 1940: 167–172). He interpreted the stone-fortified settlements along the Wadi al-Mujib corridor discussed earlier (e.g., al-Mudayna al-'Aliya, Lahun, among others), not as the agropastoralist villages that recent research has determined them to be, but rather as military outposts designed to defend the hypothetical kingdom's eastern border. Other stone towers on the eastern Karak Plateau that Glueck assumed to be part of Moab's fortification system were, in fact, constructed later, during the mid first millennium BCE, and enhanced during the Roman military's fortification of the empire's eastern border (Clark, Cocky, and Parker 2006: 39). Glueck's and others' confusion over the dates of these settlements is forgivable as they lacked today's understanding of Jordan's Iron Age ceramic vessel assemblages that are used to assign relative dates to settlement episodes.

---

military conquest over a grand primordial king during a key moment in its historical development (e.g., Stordalen 2015).

[18] Van Zyl exemplifies this acceptance of the biblical sources' characterization of Moab in his summary of the evidence (1960: notably, 4–28; 102–130).

Glueck's reconstruction of late second-millennium Moab as a politically organized kingdom has been challenged during the past few decades, beginning with critiques from Sauer (1986: 10–14) and Miller (1992). The availability of more – and more reliable – evidence through archaeological survey and excavations coupled with an increased skepticism about the trustworthiness of the biblical account of Moab's early history starting in the 1980s motivated this critique. A new-found appreciation of political evolutionary theories among Levantine archaeologists during this time also offered a framework for measuring ancient political organizations ("tribes," "chiefdoms," and "states") using archaeological evidence (LaBianca and Younker 1995). That west-central Jordan's late second-millennium BCE settlements were not organized in a detectable hierarchy in which a large administrative settlement ruled over a series of medium-size towns and smaller villages suggests Moab's political organization was less developed than the Bible's retrospective characterizations.

Despite this prevailing skepticism about early Moab's advanced political organization, Finkelstein and Lipschits have argued for an alternative scenario (Finkelstein and Lipschits 2011). Correctly casting doubt on Glueck's claim that a Moabite kingdom existed during much of the late second millennium BCE, the authors nevertheless identify an early "territorial entity" in west-central Jordan during the eleventh and tenth centuries BCE. They locate the capital of this proposed polity at Balu'a and understand the presence of its neighboring settlements (e.g., al-Mudayna al-'Aliya, al-Mudayna al-Mu'arradja) as defensive in purpose. They hypothesize that this political centralization was catalyzed by the wealth elites accumulated through its tangential participation in the copper mining industries that flourished on either side of the Wadi Arabah during these centuries (Levy, Najjar, and Ben-Yosef 2014). This territorial entity lasted until the copper industry declined in the late tenth century, a downturn Finkelstein and Lipschits attribute to the military campaigns of the Egyptian pharaoh Sheshonq I in ~926/925 BCE.

Finkelstein and Lipschits's proposal is intriguing, and should be given every consideration. Their reconstruction suffers from multiple issues, however, many of which are due to the over- and under-interpretation of the available evidence.[19] For instance, the authors argue that the archaeological and historical evidence for the second millennium, materials that were reviewed previously, is too fragmentary and under-published to interpret (Finkelstein and Lipschits 2011: 140–141).[20] While this evidence is indeed too fragmentary to satisfyingly

---

[19] To be fair, some of this evidence was unavailable to Finkelstein and Lipschits when they were developing their ideas for publication.

[20] The authors write, "To sum up, as the evidence stands today, there were no sedentary settlements south of Madaba in the Late Bronze Age and there is no unequivocal mention of Moab or

discern the region's political organization, enough documentation exists to determine that west-central Jordan saw at least limited settlement activity during the second half of the second millennium. A complete disregard of the evidence is unwarranted. An additional issue is that evidence for the prime movers that motivated the proposed "territorial entity" is absent. There is very little evidence that west-central Jordan participated in or benefited from the adjacent copper trade. Surprisingly, few copper objects have been documented in twelfth through tenth-century settlements in west-central Jordan. If these settlements were participating in the long-distance transport of copper, why were they not using the materials to craft tools and weapons?[21] A related concern is the lack of late tenth-century BCE settlement destructions that could be linked to the Egyptian pharaoh Sheshonq I campaigns east of the Jordan River in ~926/925 BCE (Finkelstein and Lipschits 2011: 147–148).

Yet the most significant issue with Finkelstein and Lipschitz's argument is the lack of evidence that would support the "territorial entity" they seek. The authors propose that Balu'a was the entity's capital based on the documentation of a fragmentary casemate wall system that is not unlike those constructed at adjacent settlements along the Wadi al-Mujib (e.g., al-Mudayna al-'Aliya). As excavations have determined in recent decades, the eleventh- and tenth-century settlement at Balu'a has been obscured by the later first millennium BCE settlement and Classical and Islamic settlements. Finkelstein and Lipschitz's claim that Balu'a is the "largest and most important site south of the Mujib" is therefore difficult to verify, in part due to preservation issues. Complicating the situation even more is the fact that the al-Mujib settlements that purportedly constituted this polity were not occupied at the same time, a point that was made earlier.

The search for an early kingdom of Moab is frustrated by the fact that the visual and extra-biblical textual evidence for political authority is problematic. A 1.83 × 1.0 m basalt stele found on the surface of Balu'a among the ruined Islamic-era village around 1930 is one such frustrating example (Crowfoot 1934; Ward and Martin 1964) (Figure 9). The stone is divided into two registers, the upper portion containing a badly damaged inscription that has yet to be deciphered (Routledge and Routledge 2009). The lower portion borrows from Egyptian visual culture to depict an investiture scene of a central unnamed figure. The lack of a known use context frustrates attempts to assign it to a particular century in Balu'a's settlement history.[22] A second frustrating

---

Moabite towns in Egyptian New Kingdom texts. The area was probably inhabited by pastoral nomads, similar to the Shasu of Edom."

[21] See Klassen and Danielson 2023 for a wide-ranging discussion on this question.
[22] See Porter 2013: 109–110 for this author's in-depth analysis of the stele.

Figure 9 The Balu'a Stele, a 1.83 × 1.0 m basalt stele. The upper register contains a badly damaged and undeciphered inscription, while the lower register contains an investiture scene borrowing from Egyptian visual culture. Found on Balu'a's surface, the precise date of the stele is unknown, but most interpreters date it to the final centuries of the second millennium BCE based on its visual elements.

example is located on a fragmentary portion of the Mesha Stele, a text that will be treated in more detail soon (Figure 9). Finkelstein, Na'aman, and Römer have recently proposed that the name of Balak, the king who sought Balaam's help in cursing the Israelites (Numbers 22–25), can be read on a (very) fragmentary line (line 31) toward the bottom of the stele (Finkelstein, Na'aman, and Römer 2019; Na'aman 2019). Using new high-resolution images of the plaster squeeze that recorded the inscription prior to its fragmentation into small pieces, the authors identify a single character – ב, the letter "B" – that they propose was the first letter of a personal name. From this single character, they offer "Balak" as a reconstruction, suggesting that ninth-century descendants of the purportedly thirteenth-century king preserved his name for four centuries and included it in the ninth-century MI. While it is an intriguing proposal, the authors themselves acknowledge their reconstruction is largely speculative.

Upon reflecting on Glueck's, Petter's, and Finkelstein and Lipshits's attempts at historical reconstructions of late second-millennium west-central Jordan, one cannot help but conclude that the textual and archaeological evidence is sufficiently ambiguous that one may arrange it any such way to produce whichever narrative fits their intellectual goals. Yet, once the problematic biblical narratives are set aside along with concerns about political classifications ("tribe" and "kingdom") and ethnic identities, the loosely affiliated agropastoralist communities that were founded and abandoned episodically across the landscape of west-central Jordan reveal a different story. Admittedly, this reconstruction is not as exciting – or newsworthy – as one that would confirm the historical reliability of the Hebrew Bible or the discovery of a "lost" biblical kingdom. This reconstruction however does align with the prevailing understanding of the broader southern Levant during the twelfth and eleventh centuries BCE as a period of political and economic recovery between New Kingdom Egypt's gradual withdrawal of their control from the region and the advent of first millennium territorial polities (Gilboa 2014). As has been well documented, the Central Highlands north and south of Jerusalem witnessed an expansion of agropastoralist villages during this interstices consisting of disaffected communities who were likely former subjects of the region's declining Canaanite city-states. The archaeological evidence found in these Central Highland villages is strikingly similar to that found in west-central Jordan, from the design of domestic residences to ceramic vessels. Therefore, a reasonable historical reconstruction of west-central Jordan would be that societies here were also responding to the political and economic vacuums of the twelfth and eleventh centuries. Hopefully, upcoming research in the region, such as the renewed excavations at Balu'a, the new excavations at Khirbat Safra, and the on-going analysis of excavated materials from previously excavated sites (e.g., al-Mudayna al-'Aliya), will offer fresh evidence that will refine our understanding of the region. Those who wish to continue their search for Sihon, Balak, Eglon, and other suspected kings may also remain cautiously optimistic, remembering that even King Mesha, a historical figure to which we now turn our attention, was once only known by a passing mention in the Hebrew Bible.

4 King Mesha's Vision of Moab

How did the politically dispersed world of second-millennium BCE agropastoralist settlements develop into the kingdom of Moab in the early first millennium? A dearth of textual and archaeological evidence from a key moment in this transition, the mid tenth to the mid ninth centuries, frustrates attempts to answer this question. A lengthy retrospective text offers some assistance in piecing together this evidentiary gap: the MI, a 1-m high basalt stone on which a first-person thirty-four-line account was authored by a Moabite king named Mesha in which he proclaimed his achievements in statecraft during the ninth century (Figure 10). Before the stele was documented in 1868 on the surface of Dhiban,[23] Mesha was only known from his brief appearance in 2 Kings 1 and 3 where it was reported that he revolted against the kingdom of Israel. The Mesha Stele's inscription contributes a considerable amount of additional information about Moab's development in the second half of the ninth century, albeit from Mesha's perspective.[24] The king begins his narrative with a short genealogy, declaring himself a resident of Dibon (Dhiban's ancient name), the king of Moab, and the successor to his father, Kemosh[yat], who ruled for three decades before him. A brief declaration follows stating that Mesha made a high place for the god Kemosh in Qarḥoh (קרחה) to thank the deity for the king's military success. The dedication of this sacred precinct, whose location has not yet been identified in Dhiban, was likely the event that catalyzed the inscription's writing. The narrative then shifts to historical matters, explaining how Kemosh's anger against the Moabites had allowed Israel's King Omri and later his unnamed son, presumedly Ahab, to control territory in the vicinity of ʿAṭarot, Madaba, Nebo, and Yahaṣ for forty years. Kemosh commanded Mesha to campaign against these settlements, enslave or slaughter their inhabitants, and destroy their temples, all of which Mesha reports he accomplished. Next, Mesha describes his building projects at Qarḥoh that benefited from the labor of campaign captives, which included fortifications, a park, a palace, reservoirs, and cisterns (lines 21–31). Additional settlements were renovated (e.g., Bet Bamot, Bezer) and new ones were reportedly founded (e.g., Baʿal-Maʿon, Qiryaten). The lower portion of the inscription is significantly damaged after

---

[23] The stele's inscription was badly damaged during the conflicts that occurred soon after its discovery in 1868. The European missionary Klein made a plaster frieze of the inscription after local Bani Hamida tribal members showed him the basalt stone. The Bani Hamida broke the stone into several pieces following European scholars' and Ottoman officials' attempts to acquire the stone. Some pieces were recovered in the ensuing decades. What is left of the stone can be viewed today at the Louvre Museum (AO 5066), although some portions are casts prepared from Klein's frieze. See Graham 1989 and Niehr and Römer 2021 for more about the stone's discovery.

[24] For translations and treatments as well as a bibliography of earlier research on the MI, see Dearman 1989; Niehr and Römer 2021; and Routledge 2004.

Figure 10 The Mesha Stele (Louvre, AP5066, https://collections.louvre.fr/en/ark:/53355/cl010120339). The light gray stone is the original preserved portion of the inscription. The black stone is a cast reconstructed from a frieze of now-lost portions of the inscription (Image: Louvre Museum).

line 31 and is broken after line 34. What can be reconstructed suggests the beginning of a new campaign narrative that was carried out in a different region, likely in the southern portions of the Karak Plateau.[25]

---

[25] Some interpreters have argued that the name David, as in the historical King David, can be read in the broken lower line 31 of the inscription (e.g., Lemaire 1994; Lemaire 2021: 154–158).

The MI remains the longest Iron Age Northwest Semitic inscription so far recovered in the Levant. Philological and historical treatments of the inscription over the past 150 years have used it to confirm and extend the biblical account of ninth-century historical events in ancient Israel and Moab (Dearman 1989). Paleographers and epigraphers draw on the text as a basis for understanding "Moabite" as a language and a script (Jackson 1989; Parker 2002). Archaeologists have used the text's geographic information to identify settlements, roads, and other features of the nascent kingdom. When using it as a source, however, the MI cannot simply be read for historical "facts." Rather, the text must be examined using a critical lens that acknowledges that it is a retrospective Ancient Near Eastern royal inscription that was commissioned by an elite patron and composed for a public audience possibly decades after the historical events it describes.[26] In other words, the text is not a dispassionate historical chronicle but rather Mesha's vision of Moab and his understanding of the roles he played as its king.[27]

A critical reading of the MI therefore sparks a number of interpretive questions that do not present clear answers. The first issue concerns whether or not Mesha's narrative can shed any light on the region north of the Wadi al-Mujib prior to Mesha's revolt, that is, during the tenth and early ninth centuries BCE. Recall from before that although Numbers 32:34 reported that the Israelite tribes of Reuben and Gad were granted territories north of the Arnon River and that Moabite territory south of the river was left intact, archaeological evidence from the twelfth and eleventh centuries does not indicate the ethnic or political identities of communities living on either side of the Wadi al-Mujib. Yet the MI suggests the political situation had changed at some point by the ninth century. Mesha describes how Israel under the Omride Dynasty governed regions north of the Arnon that Mesha understood to be Kemosh's domain, that is, "Moabite" territory. Notably, the Hebrew Bible does not describe Omri's territorial expansion east of the Jordan River prior to the reports issued in 2 Kings 1 and 3 that Mesha ended his tribute payments and revolted against Israel. These independent reports from the Hebrew Bible and the MI boost confidence in the likelihood that Israel had expanded its control east of the Jordan River

---

Some have exercised caution, however (e.g., Richelle 2021). As already mentioned, Finkelstein, Naʻaman, and Römer tentatively suggest that this fragmentary line should be reconstructed as "Balak," a Moabite king appearing in Numbers 22–25 (Finkelstein, Naʻaman, and Römer 2019; Naʻaman 2019).

[26] The MI interestingly blends the standard literary genres of the Iron Age Levantine canon. The royal inscription draws on the rhetoric of memorial genres that commemorate past achievements as well as the language of dedicatory genres that honor the gods on the occasion of newly inaugurated temples (Drinkard 1989).

[27] Hogue's thoughtful discussion of the MI and other Iron Age stele as monuments of statecraft concerned with territory is pertinent here (Hogue 2022: 354–356).

prior to the mid-ninth century. More difficult to determine, however, is exactly when Israel's expansion occurred, how long it lasted, and when it ended. The Omride Dynasty ruled Israel for nearly four decades between c. 882 and 845 BCE, with the founder Omri ruling for c. eleven years (c. 882–871 BCE), his successor Ahab ruling for c. twenty years (c. 871–852 BCE), and then Ahaziah and Jehoram, with two years and c. ten years, respectively.[28] Mesha reports in line 6 of his inscription that his revolt occurred during Omri's son's (i.e., Ahab) rule, while 2 Kings 1 and 3 clearly state that Mesha revolted *after* Ahab's death, possibly during the short two-year reign of his successor, Ahaziah, or in the early years of Jehoram's rule. The most generous duration of time for Israel's territorial domination east of the Jordan River, therefore, was approximately four decades occurring at some point between c. 885 and c. 845 BCE. If Mesha's report is accurate in line 2, the window narrows to three decades however. The inscription was therefore composed in the second half of the ninth century BCE, possibly in the century's closing decades, after some time had passed in Mesha's rule.

A related issue is the nature and extent of Israel's territorial control east of the Jordan River. Mesha reports that Omri took control of the "Land of Madaba" (lines 7–8) and Nebo (line 14), built 'Aṭarot for the "men of Gad" who had lived in the "Land of 'Aṭarot from of old" (lines 10–11), and built the town of Yaḥas (likely modern Mudayna Wadi al-Thamad) (lines 18–19). Notably, Mesha does not mention whether or not the Omrides controlled Dhiban or if it had remained under Kemoshyat's and Mesha's control throughout the ninth century BCE. So far, no substantial evidence for a tenth- or early ninth-century settlement has been documented at Dhiban beyond ceramic vessel sherds unassociated with architecture (e.g., Routledge 2004: fig. 8.5). There are some tantalizing clues in nearby settlements, however, that suggest that the Omride Dynasty may have carried out a building campaign during their rule. Finkelstein (2013: 85–103) and, separately, Edwards (2019) have observed that select settlements north of the al-Mujib share a defined set of architectural features in common with early ninth-century towns in Israel. Samaria, Hazor, and Jezreel, all major administrative towns in the kingdom of Israel, were constructed on artificial stone podia that elevated towns above the surrounding landscape. Encircling these podia were fortification systems consisting of moats, glacis, and multi-chambered gates. Similar features can be observed at 'Ataruz (ancient 'Aṭarot), Mudayna Wadi al-Thamad (ancient Yaḥaz), and al-Mukhayyat (ancient Nebo), three settlements that Mesha cites specifically as having fallen under Omride rule. Finkelstein and Edwards suggest that these repeated architectural patterns

---

[28] These dates follow Frevel 2023: Appendix 10.1.4.

indicate an Omride building program designed to strengthen major settlements under their control. While plausible, this suggestion suffers from the fact that these monumental features have not been sufficiently excavated to determine a construction date from, for instance, datable evidence in foundation trenches associated with this architecture. One notable exception may be at ʿAtaruz, where, in a limited trench in Field D, excavations documented a portion of a perimeter defensive wall. The studied wall was preserved to a height of 1 m and a width of 80 cm, and assigned a relative date to the ninth century based on ceramic vessels recovered from a "a beaten-earth floor or surface associated with the construction of the defense wall" and not a foundation trench created during the wall's construction (Ji 2011: 570).[29] This *terminus ante quem* date offers provisional evidence that the fortification was constructed prior to Mesha's mid ninth-century campaigns. Notably, Mesha also reports that he carried out a significant building campaign following his conquest of the region, making it therefore just as likely these fortifications occurred after the mid ninth century under Mesha's reign or that of one of his successors.

While more research is needed to determine the construction date of these fortification programs, the recent excavation of a temple complex at ʿAtaruz offers more secure evidence with which to answer the question of who was living in the region prior to Mesha's campaigns. Mesha mentions that the Omrides built ʿAṭarot for the "men of Gad" who had lived in the "Land of ʿAṭarot from of old," but that Mesha had attacked the town, killed the "entire population" on behalf of Kemosh, and removed their ritual equipment (lines 10–13). Excavations at ʿAtaruz have documented a temple complex that relative chronological dates from ceramic vessels suggest was founded in the late tenth or early ninth century BCE (Field Phase A7; Ji 2012: 204–205, fig. 1). The first and earliest construction phase consisted of an 8.5 × 11.5 m rectangular room with a canopy roof sheltering its western half (Figure 11). Beneath this canopy was an assortment of ritual furniture and equipment. At 10 m southwest of this room was an elevated 2.5 x 4 m platform accessed by a short staircase, a structure interpreted as an altar, possibly a *bāmāh*, an open-air high place. The second phase left the horizontal sanctuary room's perimeter in place, but subdivided it with a narrow wall running the length of the long axis (Field Phase A6; Ji 2012: 204–205, fig. 1). While this small architectural change reduced the size of the sanctuary, it also created an auxiliary room for the storage of ritual equipment, including an unhewn standing stone, a likely marker of sacred space in this context; a ceramic basin with bull protomes; a ceramic cultic stand with human and animal

---

[29] Ji assigns the wall to Stratum 9–8, the ninth century, in phase with the temple complex's second phase (Ji 2011: 570). See Section 6 for a discussion of this complex.

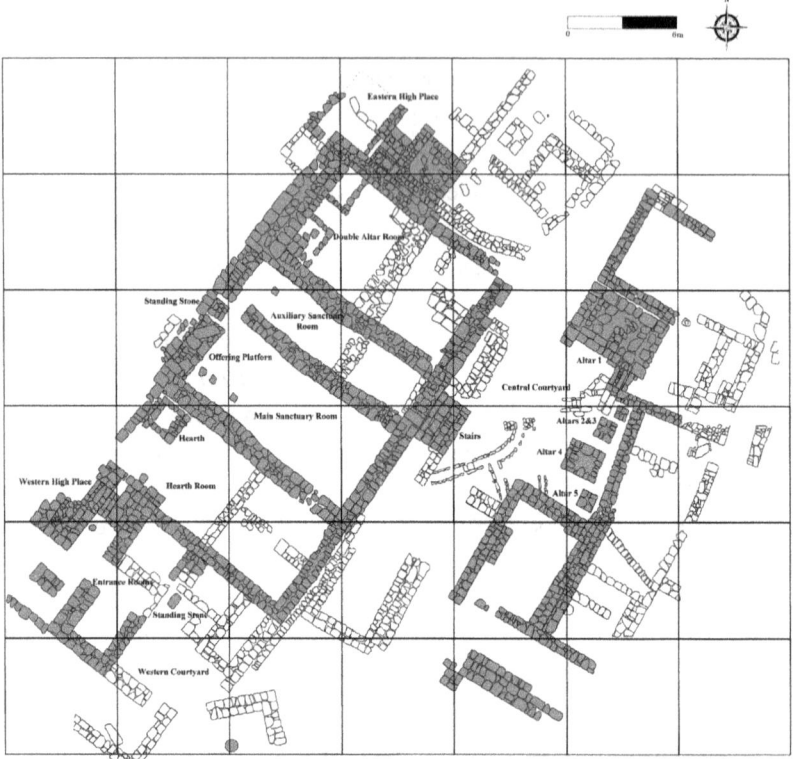

Figure 11 The 'Ataruz temple complex with the late ninth- and eighth-century architecture shaded in gray (Image: C.-H. C. Ji).

figures; and ceramic and alabaster libation vessels (Elkins 2019: 183–295; Ji 2012: 210–217; figs. 44–49). Additional horizontal rooms were constructed on either side of the sanctuary, the north room with two altars and the south room with a hearth. Three courtyards on the north, east, and south sides of this expanded temple complex hosted altars, some of which were large and tall enough to be considered *bāmôt*. A thick 5–10 cm deposit of ash sealed the floors of this second phase and buried large quantities of ritual equipment, evidence of the building's intentional destruction in the mid ninth century, approximately when Mesha claims to have destroyed 'Aṭarot in lines 11–12 of his inscription.

At some point in the second half of the ninth century BCE, likely a few decades following the temple complex's destruction, 'Ataruz was reinhabited and remained so into the early eighth century (Field Phase A5/E4; Ji 2018: 175–178; figs. 2,6).[30] In this new phase, a modest 3.2 × 4.8 m shrine was constructed

---

[30] Ji reports that the entrances to the shrine were blocked in the eighth century (Field Phase E3), a sign that the structure "peacefully" passed out of use (Ji 2018: 178).

adjacent to the destroyed temple complex containing a platform on which a small altar was built. A portable altar bearing a dedicatory inscription was found next to this platform. Noting the inscription is fragmentary, Bean and colleagues cautiously suggest a tentative reading that begins "4 + 60 from the '*brn*," followed by "4,000 foreign men were scattered, and abandoned in great number from the desolate city" (Bean et al. 2018: 229). The meaning of '*brn* is uncertain and the translators cautiously suggest the word "Hebrews" here, a term that would denote "Israel" or "Judah."[31] The shrine's adjacency to the ruined temple complex coupled with the inscription's description of conflict leads Ji, 'Ataruz's excavator, to interpret the building as a "victory shrine" commemorating Mesha's destruction of 'Ataruz. If correct, this reading strengthens the claim that the "men of Gad" affiliated with the kingdom of Israel resided in 'Ataruz. Still left unanswered, of course, is the question of when this group took up residence at 'Aṭarot.

One final matter concerns when and how the kingdom of Moab emerged. As was argued earlier, there is at present no convincing archaeological and textual evidence for a territorial kingdom in the twelfth through mid tenth centuries BCE. Yet it is clear that substantial political developments occurred south of the Wadi al-Mujib between the time that the wadi's agropastoral settlement system ended in the second half of the tenth century and Mesha's revolt c. 850 BCE, about a 75-year span of time. Mesha acknowledges his father Kemoshyat as his royal predecessor, and notes in his inscription (line 3) that he ruled over Moab for three decades. Yet because it is unknown when Mesha's rule began, it is impossible to fix in time with any precision when Kemoshyat's rule began, assuming that Mesha's claim is accurate. Nevertheless, it appears likely that Kemoshyat and, next, Mesha began their efforts to consolidate their political power across the Karak Plateau around the turn of the ninth century.

If this date is correct, the archaeological evidence for these developments is meager. No substantial settlements dating to the early ninth century BCE have so far been identified on the Karak Plateau. A likely candidate for an early capital of the fledgling polity was Karak, located on the western edge of the Plateau, a settlement that guards an important road leading down the steep cliffs to the eastern shores of the Dead Sea. Karak's likely ancient name, Kir Hareseth, is mentioned a handful of times in the Hebrew Bible, notably the prophetic

---

[31] The authors are very clear about their tentative and uncertain reading, "The cumulative effects of several cruxes ... preclude a definitive comprehensive interpretation of the inscription at this time" (216) and "Although this proposal should be considered with considerable caution, it appears to be a plausible interpretation ... ." (219). See Zadok 2020 for an alternative interpretation.

curses of Isaiah (16:7, 11) and Jeremiah (48:31, 36).[32] Kir Hareseth is also featured in the 2 Kings narrative (3:20–27) describing Moab's revolt against Israel. In their effort to bring Moab back under their control, Israel persuaded Judah and Edom to join them in a military campaign beginning on Moab's southern border. In a final battle scene, the Moabite army retreats to Kir Hareseth with their enemies in pursuit. In an act of desperation to save the town, an unnamed Moabite king, possibly Mesha, sacrifices his first-born son and offers him as a burnt offering to an unnamed god. The king's sacrifice is reported to have paid off as the invading armies were overcome by a great wrath and soon after retreated.

Any Iron Age settlement that may have existed at Karak, however, was dismantled by later building activities during the Classical, Crusader, and Islamic eras. Archaeological survey in and around the modern town, including within the Crusader and Islamic fortress that is today visible on the south end of town, has identified residual Iron Age ceramic vessel evidence attesting to a now-lost first-millennium settlement (Miller 1991: 89). Additionally, one and possibly two basalt orthostats with carved reliefs of lions' bodies were used as spolia in later Classical and Islamic era buildings (Figure 12).[33] Weber has compared these reliefs to the better-documented corpus of carved orthostats that lined the gateways and plazas of Iron Age settlements in the northern Levant (e.g., Samʻal and Zincirli), suggesting that the orthostats were displayed in similar visual programs for monumental buildings in Karak that have since been dismantled (Weber 2017). Dating the orthostats' composition to a specific century is impossible to do using the visual evidence alone, unfortunately. A dedicatory inscription found on a fragment of a likely-imported Egyptian statue mentioning Kemoshyat as the recipient was discovered around 1958 during modern building construction. Parker and Arico (2015: 115), and before them Reed and Winnett (1963), date the inscription to the mid ninth century based on paleography, and, of course, the assumption that this Kemoshyat is the same person named in line 2 of the MI. If correct, this would establish Karak under Kemoshyat's sphere of influence in the early- to mid ninth century, assuming that the object was exhibited not far from its find-spot in antiquity. Altogether, then, the fragmentary evidence from Karak requires, at best, that its status as an early capital of Moab be accepted cautiously.

---

[32] Isaiah 15:1's curse against Kir Moab, "the fortress of Moab," may also refer to Karak/Kir Hareseth.

[33] The Jabal Shihan Warrior stele is another carved basalt relief fragment found on the surface of Jabal Shihan north of Karak. See Tufnell 1953 for a description of the evidence and Hunziker-Rodewald and Deutsch 2014 for an updated interpretation.

Against Moab 37

Figure 12 Basalt orthostat with carved relief of lion's hindquarters, genitals, and tail. The orthostat was likely part of a larger program of relief sculptures in the ninth or eighth century BCE. The orthostat is located today at the Karak Archaeological Museum (Image: B. Porter).

So much for the question of where and when the political efforts to found a kingdom of Moab may have begun; now what about how? Mesha's inscription is once again the only source on the king's efforts at statecraft. The king narrates his activities according to geographical units and kin groups, some of which are designated with the term "land of" (e.g., Land of 'Aṭarot), "men of" (e.g., "Men of Gad"), or a place name (e.g., Ḥawronen). Routledge has demonstrated convincingly how this syntactical structure reflects the way Mesha spatially organized the narrative of his campaign to reflect a segmentary political hierarchy (Routledge 2004: 133–153). With Mesha's pronouncement in line 1 that he is Moab's king, he places Moab at the top of this hierarchy, signaling that all territories he now controls falls under this designation. As the narrative unfolds, however, one learns that this political entity of "Moab" consisted of multiple territorial segments that were added to the polity during the course of Mesha's campaigns. The first half of the narrative focuses on territories north of the Wadi al-Mujib and then shifts to territories south of the wadi, although this latter narrative falls at the poorly preserved bottom of the inscription. Mesha's rhetorical strategy draws on the flexible patrimonial system that was commonly practiced throughout the second and first millennium BCE that encouraged households to use kinship metaphors to reimagine themselves as members of a broader collective without sacrificing much local autonomy (Schloen 2001).

Since the Mesha Inscription's discovery in 1868, scholars have often regarded the text as a reliable source which could be productively used to reconstruct Moab's history as well as extend what is known of ancient Israel's ninth-century history. After all, unlike the Hebrew Bible, the inscription went unmolested by later redactors and, it was assumed, could offer a reliable account of the Moabite king's activities. Yet, as interpreters of ancient Near Eastern texts have grown more suspicious of the royal rhetoric of ancient kings in the past few decades, the inscription has shown itself to be a poisoned chalice that, upon a close critical reading, raises just as many questions as it offers answers. This fact must be kept in mind as we next evaluate the evidence attesting to the kingdom of Moab's brief fluorescence.

5 Locating the Kingdom of Moab

During much of the twentieth century, scholars widely assumed that Mesha's rule was the apex of Moab's political power. In the decades that followed, the kingdom was believed to have experienced a slow demise, especially when the Assyrian empire extended its power over the Levant starting in the latter third of the eighth century. Nelson Glueck, whose arguments about Iron Age Jordan's history held a convincing command over biblical scholarship for much of the century, saw this decline in the survey evidence he collected across the region (Glueck 1934: 83; 1939: 82; 1940: 139).[34] In the first extended synthesis of Moab's history, van Zyl echoed Glueck's paradigm, citing the heavy burdens of Assyrian and Babylonian vasselship placed upon the kingdom (van Zyl 1960: 144–159). Evidence from archaeological surveys and excavations collected since the 1980s has inverted Glueck's and van Zyl's paradigms, demonstrating that Mesha's mid ninth-century campaigns either coincided with or perhaps catalyzed a 250-year period of settlement intensification throughout west-central Jordan not seen since the early third millennium BCE (Philip 2008). Despite this new understanding, however, it is striking how little is still known about the kingdom's political and economic administration.

---

[34] Glueck writes, "The restoration of greater Moab marked the height of its development. Its later history was characterized by a rapid decline, which culminated in the end of Moab as an independent kingdom in the 6th century B.C." (Glueck 1940: 139). Glueck's observations that the region saw a significant drop in population between the sixth and second century, however, was correct. See Section 8 for a discussion on this later time period.

Archaeological surveys throughout west-central Jordan together demonstrate an increase in the number of settlements that started in the ninth century and continued until the late seventh and early sixth centuries before diminishing to levels that are hardly detectable in the fifth through third centuries. Surveys on the Madaba Plains identified sixty-three sites with Iron II/Persian (i.e., ninth to fifth centuries BCE) ceramics (Ibach 1987: 163; table 3.11–13; fig. 3.6), a more than 50 percent increase from the previous Iron I period ($n = 30$) (Ibach 1987: 160). Survey on the Dhiban Plateau identified fifty-three sites, an increase from nineteen sites in the Iron I period (Ji and Lee 1998, 2000), with a greater concentration of sites east of Dhiban compared to the area west of the settlement (Ji 2007: 141). Survey on the Karak Plateau identified ninety-eight ninth- to eighth-century settlements; five or more ceramic sherds were discovered at twenty-eight of those settlements (Miller 1991: 309–310).[35] While this evidence attests to the widespread settlement activity that occurred across the region, accessing these settlements through excavations is perennially challenged by later first and second millennia CE construction activity that has obscured the Iron Age evidence. Nowhere has this settlement erasure been more dramatic, as was already noted, than Karak, where the Classical, Crusader, and Islamic era occupations erased whatever existed of ancient Kir Hareseth, what may have been Moab's earliest capital. A similar issue persists at Dhiban, ancient Dibon, although archaeologists have had more success documenting the Iron Age settlement and nearby necropolis (Morton 1989; Porter et al. 2007, 2010, 2012: 120–125; Routledge 2013; Tushingham 1972; Winnett and Reed 1964) (Figure 13). Ancient Dhiban likely spanned two hills: although the northern one is only available for excavation today, the other being the location of the modern settlement. It is on this southern 12 ha tell that the MI is believed to have been located on the surface of the southeast corner when the Bani Hamida tribe first showed it to a European missionary in 1868. This assumption is what led the site's first investigators to focus their work in this specific place in hopes of identifying structures that Mesha had described in lines 21–24 of his inscription: "I built Qarḥoh, the wall of the wood lot and the wall of the acropolis, and I built the palace ... ." Excavations in the southeast corner identified components of a fortification system consisting of a retaining wall, at least one tower, and a monumental wall that was battered at an angle of c. 15 degrees (Figure 14) (Tushingham 1972: 5–26; Plan 2; Winnett and Reed 1964: 43).[36] An artificial fill of materials up to 10 m deep in some places was located

---

[35] See also Parker 2006 for the eastern edge; Worschech 1985 for the northwest corner; and Mittmann 1981 and Jacobs 1983 for the southwest corner of the Karak Plateau.

[36] The corners of a likely gate were identified on the northeast corner of the site (Area H; Morton 1989: fig. 4) in addition to these fortifications identified on the south-east corner.

Figure 13 Tall Dhiban looking west, March 2024. (Tall Dhiban ©APAAME-20240304_FB-0007. Image: R. Bewley).

just behind these structures. This fill was part of a major ninth- or eighth-century construction project designed to enlarge the settlement artificially by at least 0.75 ha (Tushingham 1990; Tushingham and Pedrette 1995). This building project created a podium to support what may have been substantial structures that were later replaced by Classical and Islamic periods buildings.

A large rectangular building at least 20 m wide and 40 m long was identified on the summit of the south hill (Figure 15) (Morton 1989: 244–246; fig. 13). Figurines, an incense stand, and a seal impression on a jar were identified in the building's eleven small rooms (Morton 1989: 243–246; figs. 9–12, 14–16). These objects along with the building's monumental walls evoke the building's possible elite status, leading Morton to label the building a "palace" and ascribe it to Mesha's building program. The king listed the construction of a *bt mlk* (בת מלך), a "house of the king," a common term for "palace," in line 23 of his inscription. Routledge's reanalysis of Morton's plans, notes, and recovered ceramic vessels refined Morton's assessment, identifying four distinct phases of use (Routledge 2004: 161–168; Table 8.1). The first phase was dated to the mid ninth century and consisted of plaster floors located above a construction fill containing ceramic vessels dating to the third and second millennia.[37]

---

[37] Radiocarbon testing of a barley seed from this phase yielded a calendar date of 770–553 cal BCE (2σ 2511 +/- 30 BP; OxA-23575). This broad temporal range is due to the Hallstatt Plateau phenomenon that prevents radiocarbon dates from being precise during the first half of the first

Against Moab 41

Figure 14 Southeast corner of Dhiban's fortification system looking east. The lowest courses date to the first millennium BCE with Classical and Islamic structures built above them. This area has seen excavation and cleaning in recent years (Image: B. Porter).

A second phase marked by a surface indicated that a renovation occurred in the late eighth or early seventh century, around the time when Moab's relationship with the Assyrian empire began. Fill deposits above this surface dating to the late seventh century indicates that the building went out of use at some point during this century, a pattern seen throughout the site. Recent excavations of intact deposits within this building confirmed Routledge's interpretation of Morton's phasing and dating of the building (Figure 16) (Porter et al. 2010: 28–30; figs. 15–18, 2012: 120–125). With this corroboration of the building's ninth-century construction date, it is tempting to attribute it to Mesha's building campaign, a fact that is admittedly difficult to verify in the absence of a dedicatory inscription or archive. What is visible of the building's design – a series of rectangular rooms of various sizes – does find comparison with other ninth- and eighth-century monumental buildings in the southern Levant, such as Lachish (Levels IV-III; Ussishkin 2004: 78–90; 777–840; figs. 14.8–9) and "Omri's Palace" at Samaria (Reisner, Fisher, and Gordon 1924: 98–114; pl. 5).[38] Unfortunately, attempts to document additional

---

millennium BCE. Relative dates from ceramic vessels provide more narrow and accurate dates for this time period.
[38] See Reich 1992: 203–210 for an overview of Iron Age palaces from the neighboring kingdoms of Israel and Judah.

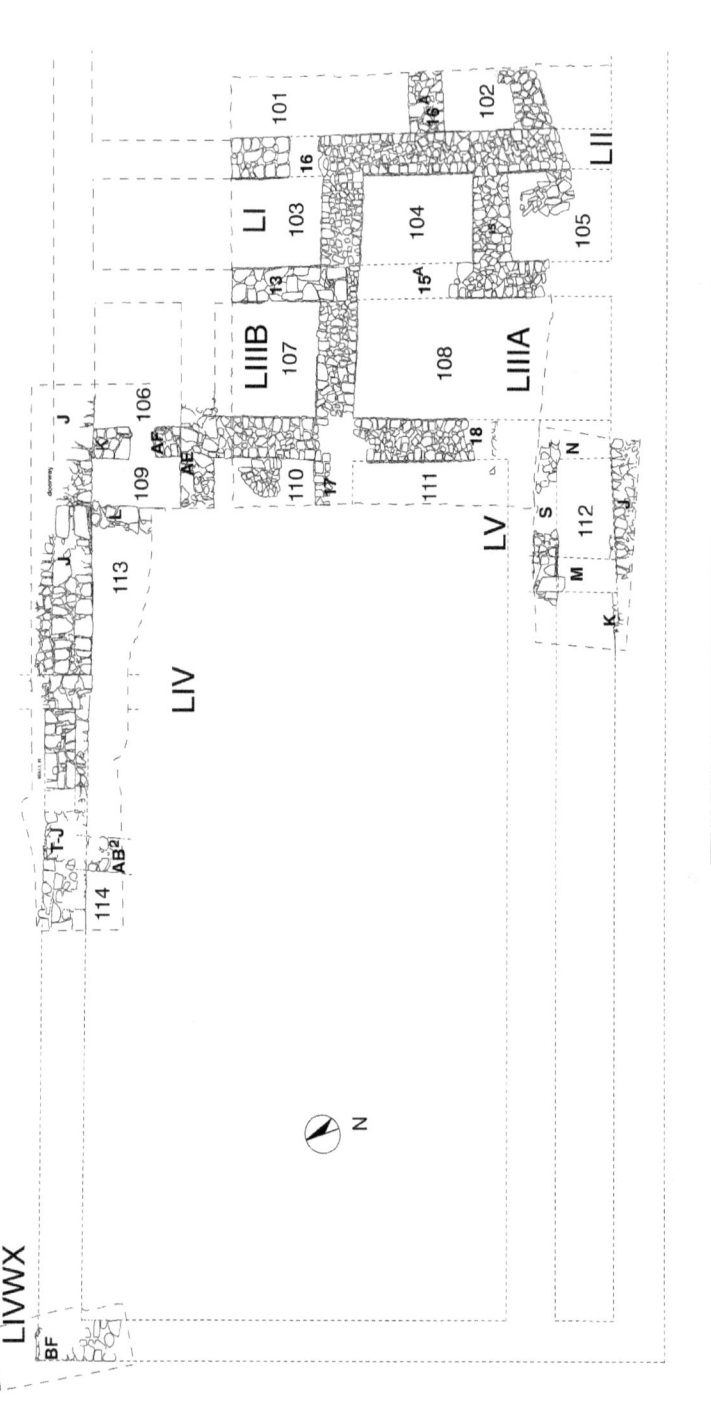

Figure 15 A rectangular monumental building located at the summit of Dhiban's southern tell. The building is at least 20 m long and 40 m wide. Morton, the building's excavator, coined the building "Mesha's palace," although this attribution is impossible to verify at this time. Recent excavations have dated the construction of this building to the ninth century BCE (Image: B. Routledge).

Figure 16 A stratigraphic section illustrating different construction phases of Dhiban's monumental building based on excavations carried out in 2009. Three successive surfaces were identified (Loci 24, 18, and 12) that dated between the ninth and seventh centuries BCE. These results corroborated Morton's observations about the building's different phases (Image: B Porter).

architecture west of Morton's building was unsuccessful; Late Antique and Middle Islamic construction activities removed all Iron Age architecture. Iron Age evidence is possibly preserved to the south of the exposed architecture, however.

Mesha also described in lines 23–26 of his inscription how he constructed Dhiban's hydrological infrastructure, "And I made the retaining walls of the reservoir for the [spring] inside the city.[39] And there were no cisterns inside the city at Qarḥoh and I said to all the people 'Make for yourselves each a cistern in his house.' And I dug the ditches for Qarḥoh with prisoners of Israel." These construction projects were likely necessary to sustain a larger population in the semi-arid environment of the Dhiban Plateau. Excavations at Dhiban have documented dozens of cisterns scattered throughout the site that were likely created and used during the first millennium BCE. Excavations on the western edge of the site identified an open water reservoir that captured run-off precipitation from the adjacent slope (Figure 17) (Routledge 2013). A stone wall was built adjacent to a natural depression in the bedrock. Ceramic vessels found in the reservoir dated to the tenth and ninth centuries BCE, suggesting that the feature was in use during and slightly after Mesha's building program. More hydrological features likely remain to be discovered in and on the perimeter of Dhiban.

Given that the MI was discovered at Dhiban, it is retrospectively understandable why scholars began their investigations into the kingdom there, despite the fact that first millennium BCE evidence was difficult to access and obscured by later settlements. Additional sites in the region have seen systematic archaeological excavations with mixed results, such as the cluster of settlements that reside in the Madaba Plains north of Dhiban. According to archaeological surveys in and around Madaba that mapped the distribution of Iron Age II ceramic sherds found on the surface, Madaba may have reached a staggering 13–16 ha in the ninth and eighth centuries (Harrison 1997: 140). This estimate has not been tested through excavation and a more modest size is likely, but if accurate, Madaba would be the largest first millennium settlement in western Jordan. On the modern town's acropolis, excavations have documented a stone fortification wall that is 5 m high, 7 m wide, and has so far been documented over 30 m in length (Harrison 2009: 34; fig. 2). The date of the wall's construction is unknown, but multiple expansion phases are visible in what has been left for discovery, at least two of which occurred in the early centuries of the first millennium. "Madaba" has been proposed for a lacuna in a list of place names in line 30 of the MI that the king claims he built.[40] Three phases, each with built structures of varying quality, were identified east, or inside, the wall (Foran et al. 2004: 79–82; Harrison 2009: 36–37). A large pillared building made up Field

---

[39] "Spring" here is a reconstruction from a broken word, *[lm']yn*. While translators agree that the word is likely associated with "water," there are disagreements with the precise rendering. See Lemaire 2021: 161 for a rendering of "réservo[ir d']eau" and Routledge 2013: 52 for additional discussion on this passage.

[40] Most translators will logically restore בא[...] as "Madaba" in line 30 (e.g., Dearman 1989: 95; Routledge 2004: 135–136). Lemaire reconstructs *[bt.mhd]b* or "temple of Madaba."

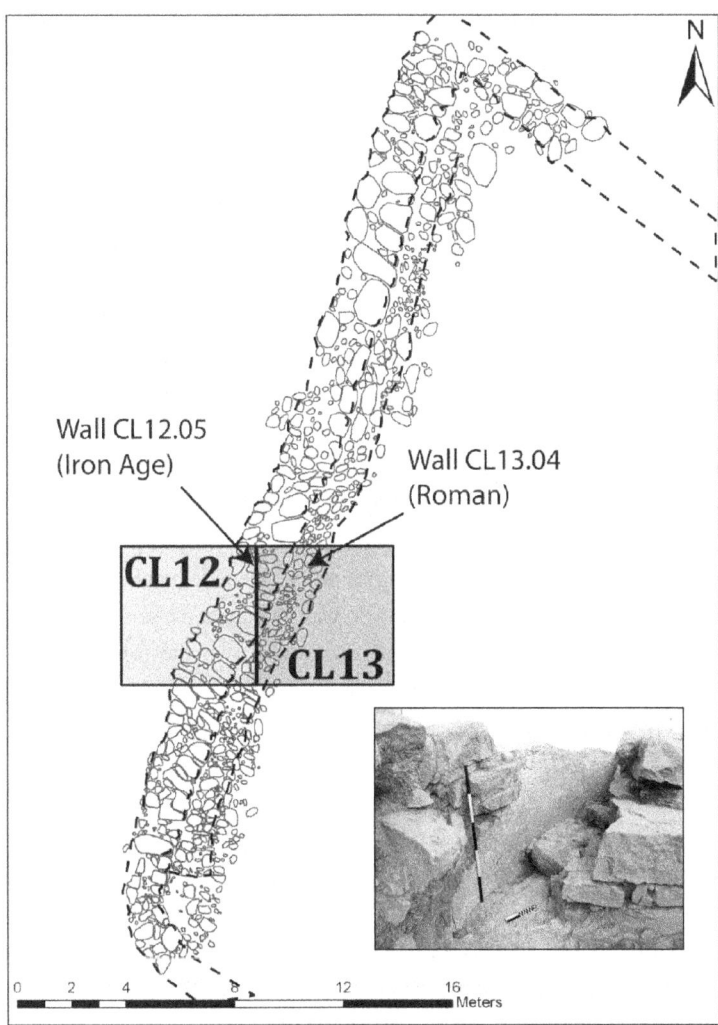

Figure 17 A water reservoir located on the west side of Dhiban. Wall CL.12.05 was constructed in the first millennium. The structure was then widened and repaired in the later Classical Era. (Image: B. Routledge).

Phase 8 that dated to the ninth century BCE according to radiocarbon dates (Harrison and Barlow 2005). Beneath this building, a fragmentary monumental building was detected in an early phase (Phase 9). Above the Phase 8 pillared building, a so-called squatter settlement consisting of ephemeral structures was documented. Like Dhiban, there is little evidence that Madaba was occupied in the seventh century aside from the discovery of arbitrary sherds. While the excavated results from Madaba are narrowly defined due to the ancient settlement's location under the modern city, what has been documented suggests

Madaba was a substantial settlement possibly before, but certainly after Mesha's campaign and his successors' rule.

Multiple sites exist in Madaba's vicinity where ninth- and eighth-century settlements are suspected. Many have yet to be documented in full or the evidence is too obscure to characterize the settlement in any detail. At Hisban, Strata 17 (Iron IIB) and 16 (Iron IIC/Persian) consisted of rich fill deposits in and around a large cistern containing ceramic vessels and objects dating between the late tenth and sixth centuries (Ray 2001: 121–155). To the west of Madaba is Khirbat al-Mukhayyat, ancient Nebo, where systematic excavations have only recently begun to detect first millennium evidence. Research has so far determined that the settlement's monumental fortifications were in use during the late eighth and seventh centuries, but were likely founded a century or two earlier (Field C; Danielson and Foran 2021: 99–100). Tell al-Mashhad, located north of al-Mukhayyat in Wadi 'Ayun Musa, was a small horizontal settlement perched on a hilltop above the spring that was settled between the eighth and sixth centuries BCE (Benedettucci 2022: fig. 168). A rectangular structure, possibly a tower, was located at the settlement's highest point, with thin fortification walls descending down the topography. Small buildings are located within these walls in a design that is not unlike what was seen in the Wadi al-Mujib settlement system examined earlier.

To the southwest of Madaba is 'Ataruz, ancient 'Aṭarot, where excavations have determined that the town was founded as early as the late tenth century and as late as the early ninth century. The settlement was destroyed in the mid ninth century, possibly during Mesha's campaign against the town, and was resettled soon after (Ji 2011; Ji and Bates 2017). The town declined or was abandoned toward the end of the eighth or the beginning of the seventh century. Excavations have so far concentrated on the fortification system and the temple complex that were described in Section 4. East of 'Ataruz and Dhiban is Mudayna Wadi al-Thamad, likely ancient Yaḥaz, a settlement already discussed and will be discussed again soon. It is difficult to determine what role the settlement played in the ninth and eighth centuries, as much of what has been so far reported from excavations dates to the seventh and sixth centuries BCE (Chadwick et al. 2024).

Karak was not the only large ninth- and eighth-century settlement on the plateau. About 20 km to the north-east of the possible capital was Balu'a, a settlement estimated to be 16 ha in size.[41] The settlement was constructed

---

[41] As was noted earlier, the site had witnessed occupation in the eleventh century and was one of the settlements included in the Wadi al-Mujib agropastoralist settlement system. Settlement activity in the Hellenistic Nabataean and Middle Islamic Periods have obscured earlier settlement activity in some areas of Balu'a. Excavations recently resumed at Balu'a and will likely yield new evidence for refining this understanding of the settlement's history and organization.

on the edge of a cliff whose steep drop offered a natural fortification for the town. A 7-m-wide casemate fortification wall was documented on what was likely the settlement's eastern perimeter (Bramlett, Vincent, and Ninow 2018: 62; Roddy, Bramlett, and Ninow 2024; Worschech 1995). This wall may have been part of a larger system that enveloped the settlement's upper city, although additional research is needed to determine the full extent of this fortification system. A rectangular monumental stone building, known colloquially as the "*qasr*," sits near the settlement's center and is preserved at a height of 7 m in some places. Recent excavations of the exterior of the northern wall confirmed the building's use in the ninth and eighth centuries (Bramlett, Vincent, and Ninow 2018: 2).[42] To the east of the qasr, a fragment of a basalt volute capital was identified as spolia in a Hellenistic Nabataean altar (Tyson and Ninow 2019). These capitals have been identified around the southern Levant, including west-central Jordan at Mudaybi' (Drinkard 1997), 35 km to the southeast of Balu'a, and are assumed to have been ornamental architectural elements used in elite settings (Lipschits 2011; Shiloh 1979).

'Ataruz, Balu'a, Dhiban, Madaba, al-Mukhayyat, and their neighbors were substantial population centers in the ninth and eighth centuries BCE. Smaller settlements also existed, often located along the major roads that connected settlements with each other. These smaller settlements appear to have played a defensive role in monitoring traffic. An ~18 m^2 tower was constructed on a road running between 'Ataruz and Libb, a site in which surface surveys have documented first-millennium BCE ceramic vessels (Ji 2016: 219). The site's purpose was to monitor this important road, a tributary of the King's Highway. Rescue excavations of the damaged site determined that it consisted of a podium preserved in places 3.5 m high and attached buildings that may have served as residences (Ji 2016: 218). The buildings were constructed in the early ninth century and continued to be used through the seventh century, dates that were assigned based on ceramic vessel evidence (Ji 2016: fig. 7). Another possible defensive settlement is 'Aro'er, located on the edge of the Wadi al-Mujib, southeast of Dhiban. Mesha describes that he built 'Aro'er and made a highway through the Arnon (line 26), a pairing that suggests the settlement was designed to monitor a highway connecting the Dhiban and Karak Plateaus. Excavations at 'Aro'er detected an ~50 m^2 fortified building constructed on the canyon's rim that was assigned to Level IV and dated to the ninth and eighth centuries (Olávarri 1965, 1969, 1993). Confirming the date of this structure is challenging as the published ceramic vessel forms easily date to those found in

---

[42] Notably, late second millennium BCE ceramic sherds were found in lower deposits, suggesting a *terminus ante quem* date for the building (Bramlett, Vincent, and Ninow 2018: 2).

the eleventh- and tenth-century settlements of the Wadi al-Mujib settlements already discussed (Olávarri 1965: fig. 2).[43] This rather modest site is mentioned frequently in the Hebrew Bible and the text often notes its location next to the Arnon (e.g., Joshua 12:2; Joshua 13:9, 16; 2 Kings 10: 32–33). According to the excavator, the building shows no sign of use during the seventh century, a possible indication that the canyon's crossing point had shifted east to Lahun.

The survey and excavation evidence unquestionably attest to an intensification in sedentary settlement in west-central Jordan starting in the ninth century and continuing into the eighth century. This demographic change conspicuously begins during Mesha's rule in the late ninth century, suggesting that the king's military and building campaigns possibly catalyzed an uptick in sedentary life. Yet, beyond this knowledge of the timing of this intensification and the construction of public architecture that supported the kingdom's regional administration, the question of how these settlements were organized into a regional political and economic administration is difficult to answer. Were Dhiban and Karak presumedly seats of political power that oversaw their neighboring settlements, such as 'Ataruz, Balu'a, Madaba, al-Mukhayyat, and others? Mesha's presentation of the segmentary organization of west-central Jordan's political landscape would suggest that such an arrangement was plausible, but no study has occurred. A related question is how best to envision the kingdom's economic organization during the ninth and eighth centuries BCE. Mesha describes in his inscription how he carried out infrastructure projects in his newly won territory that assumedly created the material conditions for a viable regional economy. Did households scale their output to meet their subsistence requirements, contribute to palace and temple coffers, and exchange any remaining surplus in local markets? The admittedly thin corpus of evidence available to characterize Moab's regional organization suggests the kingdom was arranged into a loosely integrated political hierarchy supported by a royal redistributive economy. This hardly satisfying characterization calls out for additional research on this important period in Moab's development.

6 Beyond the Kemosh Cult

Mesha's adoration of Kemosh in his inscription suggests that the deity's cult played a role in the king's efforts at statecraft. Yet just who this Kemosh was and how he came to be so important to Mesha is unknown. Possible variant

---

[43] Knowledge of first millennium ceramic vessel assemblages was limited during the years in which Olávarri excavated 'Aro'er. If the excavated evidence were ever to be located, a reanalysis of the results would be in order.

spellings of the god's name may be present in much earlier texts in Syria, at Ebla in the third millennium, and later, at Ugarit in the late second millennium BCE.[44] If these textual attestations indeed reflect an early Kemosh cult in the northern Levant, there is no evidence that could describe how the deity rose to prominence in first-millennium BCE Jordan. The Hebrew Bible, where Kemosh appears in eight instances affiliated with Moab, is also mute on the deity's origin story.[45] Kemosh's relationship with Moab has been understood through the theological framework presented in the Hebrew Bible and other ancient Middle Eastern sources in which a deity establishes a patrimonial covenant with a king and his constituents. In such agreements, humans obey, honor, and sacrifice to the deity in exchange for its protection. The biblical writers presented Levantine kingdoms as participants in these patrimonial relationships with select deities much as Israel and Judah did with their gods. Mesha's description of his relationship with Kemosh throughout his inscription confirms Moab's kings participated in a similar practice. Kemosh is described with characteristics typical of first millennium Northwest Semitic deities, a god who will protect and support loyal worshippers, but can also withdraw its support with devastating consequences. Mesha describes in line 5 of his inscription that Kemosh's anger with Moab led him to punish the kingdom by allowing Israel to occupy Moab's territory. Yet after a period of time, Kemosh commands Mesha to carry out his campaigns against Israel, offering Moab's military his celestial support.

Mesha's inscription also reveals the enduring importance of Kemosh and his cult to Moab's ruling dynasty. Kemosh's name is included as a theophoric element in the names of three kings: Kemoshyat in line 1 of the MI and in line 1 of the Karak Inscription, the late eighth-century king Kammusunadbi, and the seventh-century king Kamashḥalta in Assyrian records, which will be discussed next. Personal names in the ancient Middle East often included theophoric elements that signaled the bearer's (or their parents') piety toward that deity (Albertz and Schmitt 2012: 245–386; Benz 1972; Tigay 1986). Mesha's inscription also mentions that he dedicated a temple at Nebo to the deity 'Ashtar-Kemosh in line 17, a hint that a deity 'Ashtar was assimilated into the Kemosh cult (Snyder 2010: 648).

---

[44] The evidence for Kemosh at Ebla, Ugarit, and possibly Karkemish is summarized thoroughly in Jang 2009: 47 and Ray 2003: 7–8. Cornell summarizes the evidence for Kemosh's shadowy continuity in the latter half of the first millennium BCE (2016). Note, especially, his review of the discussion surrounding the Hellenistic reception of Kemosh as Ares, the Greek god of war (11–12).

[45] E.g., Numbers 21:29; Judges 11:24; 1 Kings 11:7; 11:33; 2 Kings 23:13; and Jeremiah 48. To take but one example, the prophet Jeremiah proclaims, "Moab shall be ashamed because of Kemosh" (48: 13). The Hebrew Bible also reports many episodes where Moabites are engaged in some form of ritual worship or activity. These episodes have served as sources for describing Moabite "religion" (Jang 2009; Mattingly 1989; Ray 2003).

The MI also reports that the king carried out one of the most important acts of piety for a Levantine king: the construction of temples which acted as "houses" for the deity where worshippers offered prayers and sacrifices. In lines 29–30, Mesha reports that he built temples at Ba'al Ma'on and Diblaten, two towns whose locations were likely in the vicinity of Madaba,[46] a third town that is probably mentioned in this fragmentary list of building activities. The inscription's rhetoric, however, singles out the commemoration of Mesha's construction of one particular sacred space, Qarḥoh, as the inscription's *raison d'être*, an act of gratitude to thank Kemosh for his guidance during Mesha's campaigns. Mesha boasts on line 3, "I made this high place (הבמת; *hbmt*) for Kemosh in Qarḥoh." This term *bāmāh* appears multiple times in the Hebrew Bible to describe large elevated presumably outdoor altars where sacrifices of incense and other materials were offered (Barrick 1991). The Judahite prophet Isaiah describes a *bāmāh* located somewhere in Dhiban in one of his prophecies against Moab: "Dibon has gone up to the temple, to the high places to weep" (Isaiah 15:2). So far, no evidence for a structure that might resemble an altar has been documented by past or current excavation projects. A very small 5 cm² fragmentary inscription incised in basalt, not unlike the stone on which the MI was carved, was found on Dhiban's surface in 1951. While the upper register of letters is too obscure to make any confident reading, the three successive letters, בת . כ, on the bottom row have been reconstructed by some as *bt . k* [*mš*], "house of Kemosh" or "temple of Kemosh" (Murphy and Carl 1952). Obviously, the reconstruction of Kemosh's name based on a single letter is speculative. One other possible mention of an earlier temple to Kemosh appears in the second line of an inscribed statue fragment from Karak dating to Kemoshyat's reign. The beginning of line 2 is broken, כמש . ת[...], and has often been reconstructed as [*b*]*t . kmš*. A much-later late fourth-century Aramaic inscription found in Karak, the Sarra' Inscription, mentions a temple to Kemosh, raising the possibility that whatever sacred complex Kemoshyat had constructed in the ninth century may have lasted through the centuries (Milik 1958–1959).

While this evidence suggests that Kemosh's cult was widely shared across west-central Jordan, other deities appear to have been worshipped in the region (Mattingly 1989: 216–227). In line 18 of his inscription, Mesha describes how he removed the "vessels of Yahweh" from Nebo and brought them before Kemosh, an acknowledgement that the (Israelite?) god had been worshipped

---

[46] See Dearman 1989 for a discussion of possible locations based on historical geography. Diblaten may be modern Libb or the Roman settlement Umm al-Rasas, and Ba'al Ma'on may be modern Ma'in, southwest of Madaba.

in the region prior to Mesha's conquest. The names of a handful of settlements listed in the MI and the Hebrew Bible contain theophoric elements for deities such as Ba'al,[47] Horon,[48] and Nabu, a Mesopotamian deity associated with wisdom.[49] The names of these and other deities (e.g., 'El) also appear in personal names on incised stamp seals, stone objects on which short texts and images were carved, found in west-central Jordan or affiliated with the region.[50] One should also not completely disregard the biblical writers' statements that Moabites worshipped multiple deities (e.g., Numbers 25:1–5; Judges 10:6; Jeremiah 48:35; Ruth 1:15).

When considered together, the MI, the biblical sources, and the fragmentary epigraphic evidence point to the likelihood that multiple deities were worshipped in west-central Jordan and, following from that, it was necessary for Mesha and his successors to promote and sustain Kemosh's cult. Yet it remains to be determined how successful these efforts in fact were. This is a key question to answer as the cult was one of the royal family's instruments to promote their rule over west-central Jordan. The large assemblage of first-millennium BCE incised stamp seals serve as a proxy for understanding how individuals across west-central Jordan self-fashioned their pietistic identities (Avigad and Sass 1997: 372–386; Eggler and Keel 2006).[51] Egyptian and Mesopotamian visual themes often inspired the images that were incised in these stones. Ritual scenes sometimes appear with worshipper and altar in the presence of deities signified by celestial bodies, usually moons and stars, understood to be the deities Nin and Ištar, respectively, when found in a Mesopotamian context.[52] In a Levantine setting, however, these icons were likely understood as local deities with which the owner would have familiarity. Some seals display short inscriptions with names or short honorific statements containing theophoric elements. Using

---

[47] For instance, the settlement Ba'al Ma'on, likely Ma'in, is mentioned on line 30 of the MI and Ba'al Pe'or appears in Numbers 25 and Deuteronomy 3:29.

[48] The settlement Hawronen is mentioned in line 32 of the MI, and in Jeremiah 48:3 and Isaiah 15:5. The location of Hawronen is unclear but see Ben-David 2001 for a summary of the debate and relevant bibliography.

[49] Nebo, mentioned in line 14 of the MI and in several passages in the Hebrew Bible (e.g., Deuteronomy 34:1; Numbers 32:3).

[50] See Albertz and Schmitt 2012: Table 5.9 for a complete list of 42 personal names. However, Snyder cautions that theophoric elements under consideration here also could serve as generic terms denoting a "god" and that a specific deity cannot be determined. In one instance, Kemosh and 'El even appear together as כמשאל, "Kmšel," "Kemosh is god." (Avigad and Sass 1997: 374; no. 1010). See also Timm 1989: 159 ff for an alternative discussion of the evidence.

[51] These objects are commonly recovered in archaeological contexts, but are also identified in private collections, the unfortunate result of site looting and trafficking across international borders. In the latter case, provenience at the site level is impossible to verify.

[52] See, e.g., Avigad and Sass 1997: 379, no. 1027; 380, nos. 1031 and 1035.

Avigad and Sass's corpus (Avigad and Sass 1997),[53] Snyder counted twelve out of forty-two seals sourced from west-central Jordan bearing a Kemosh element (Snyder 2010: 648; Appendix A), a suggestion that persons with access to stamp seals exercised a degree of personal piety toward Kemosh.

The three intriguing ritual contexts that have been documented north of the Wadi al-Mujib unfortunately cannot be affiliated with the Kemosh cult, or, in fact, any deity's cult.[54] Yet this evidence does illuminate the types of ritual activities that were practiced during the ninth and eighth centuries BCE and therefore deserves careful examination. The first context was documented on 'Ataruz's acropolis that was already described. Recall that Ji, the excavator, interpreted the context as a late ninth- and early eighth-century victory shrine commemorating the destruction of the nearby ruined temple, an event that may also be mentioned in the MI (lines 10–14) (Ji 2012, 2018). In Field Phase E4, the sanctuary consisted of a small 4.9×4.8 m room with an approximately 1.7×3.9 m platform on which a small cuboid altar was placed (Figure 18) (Ji 2018: 175–178). Facing the platform were three stone slabs that likely served as offering tables. No benches were identified in the room. Two altars, one bearing an inscription that was described in Section 4 (Bean et al. 2018), and a cup-and-saucer stand, were found between the platform and the tables, a suggestion that the equipment had originally been situated on the platform (Ji 2018: figs. 4, 5, 13). In the middle of the eighth century (Field Phase E3), the entrances into the sanctuary was blocked, signaling the possibility that the ritual context was peacefully decommissioned.

A second ritual context was documented at Mudayna Wadi al-Thamad located 24 km southeast of 'Ataruz (Chadwick et al. 2024: 138–147; Daviau and Steiner 2000; Dion and Daviau 2000). Excavations on the northern edge of the town documented a monumental gate that served as the town's primary entrance. Just inside the gate was Building 149, a small stone building that contained an approximately 30 m^2 room (Figure 19) (Daviau and Steiner 2000: figs. 2, 6). Low benches covered with white- or red-tinted plaster were built around much of the room's perimeter. The room was also divided by another low bench with pillars built on either side that supported the room's ceiling. The objects recovered in the room, which included stone altars and ceramic objects,

---

[53] Avigad and Sass's classification is challenged by the fact that several examples lack an archaeological provenience. Some examples are defined as "Moabite" based on their visual or paleographic qualities.

[54] Not to be forgotten is the so-called Nebo shrine group which was purchased on the antiquities market and now resides in the Museum of Art and Archaeology at the University of Missouri, Columbia (Weinberg 1978). The assemblage consists of ritual equipment including a model shrine, ceramic animal rhyta, a horse figurine, and multiple ceramic vessels. A reexamination of this assemblage in light of new knowledge about Iron Age Levantine ritual practices is needed.

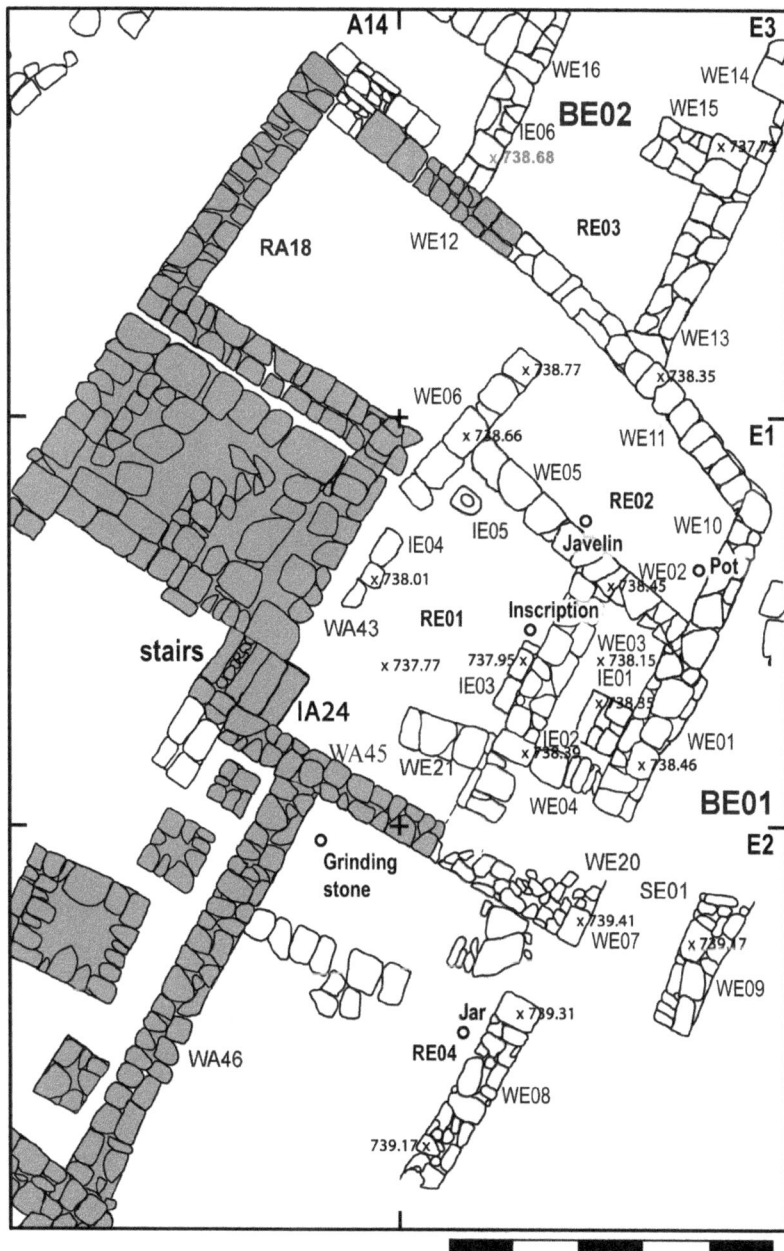

Figure 18 Temple Building E01 at Khirbat 'Ataruz. The sanctuary was 4.9 × 4.8 m room containing a platform on which small altars were placed. Ji, the excavator, interprets the ritual space as a victory shrine commemorating Mesha's conquest of the settlement (Image: C.H. Ji).

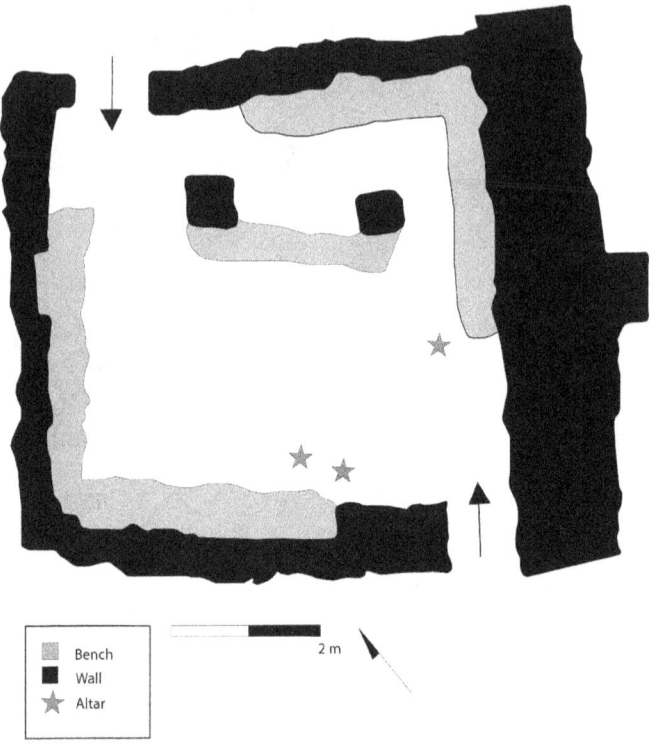

Figure 19 Sanctuary 149 at Mudayna Wadi al-Thamad (Reworked after Daviau and Steiner 2000: figs. 2 and 6).

notably lamps and figurines, speak to the room's ritual purpose (Daviau and Steiner 2000: figs. 7–13). Many of these objects were located in a pit (R108) in the room's southern half. The use of Building 149 ended following what appears to have been a violent destruction in which these ritual objects were abandoned, an event that probably coincided with the settlement's destruction by the Babylonian Empire in the early sixth century BCE.

Portable altars played an important role in the ritual activities that took place in the 'Ataruz temple and Mudayna Wadi al-Thamad's Building 149. The altars were platforms where offerings of liquid libations and incense were made to deities while having a recursive sensorial affect on the worshipper's experience. Altar 4/11 at Mudayna Wadi al-Thamad, for instance, was designed to receive libations that may have included olive oil, wine, perfumes, and animal fats (Figure 20) (Daviau and Steiner 2000: 8–10; figs. 7–8). The altar is quadrangular in shape and divided into two sections. The lowest portion of the bottom section was broken and not recovered. Enough is preserved of the lower section, however, to observe "legs" carved in relief, in an attempt to give the object

Figure 20 Two altars found inside Sanctuary 149 at Mudayna Wadi al-Thamad (Reworked after Daviau and Steiner 2000: fig. 6).

a sense of being free-standing. The upper half presents itself as a block sitting on top of this imagined "stand." The upper register of the block has red and black pigments preserved on one side of the object. The altar's platform is surrounded by a border that varies between 4 and 6 cm thick. In one quadrant of the platform is a circular depression that is incised to allow liquids to drain from the platform. The depression's location is conspicuously located on the same corner as a circular design element that sits below it. The depression suggests the altar's intended function was for liquid offerings made to some unknown deity.[55]

Not all portable altars were designed in a similar way nor had the same purpose of receiving libations. The inscribed altar from 'Ataruz discussed earlier as well as a second inscribed altar from Mudayna Wadi al-Thamad, 4/15, are different in shape and design from Altar 4/11. The altar is almost 1 m in height and is divided into six registers, consisting of narrow prismatic-shaped

---

[55] A second smaller stone altar called 4/14 was found nearby (Daviau and Steiner 2000: 10; fig. 8b). The platform sloped toward its middle where ash and soot was preserved, indicating that burning activities had occurred on the surface.

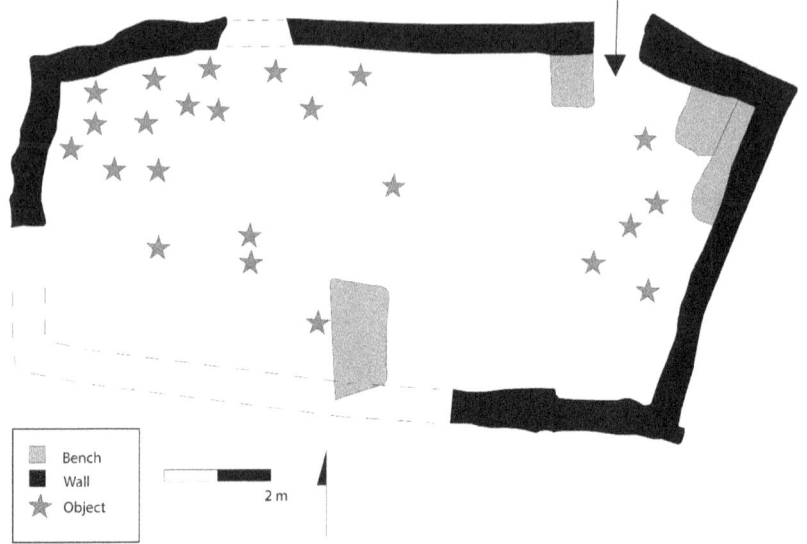

Figure 21 Shrine at WT-13 illustrating the find spots of objects inside the building (Reworked after Daviau 2017a: 61; fig 3.26b).

sections that support three rounded sections. Each register is divided by a line of carved drooping petals that were painted red and black interchangeably. The highest section is carved out on the top to create a bowl in which soot was found. The altar's publication reports the presence of a palm tree-shaped design, but it is difficult to discern from photographs and drawings. On the same register on the near opposite side of this pigment is a two-line twenty-two-character Northwest Semitic inscription incised into the object's side. Dion translates the lines as "The *mqṭr* that Elishama made for *ysp*, the daughter of *'wt*." Here, the name of a maker or sponsor, Elishama, is noted who made the object for a woman, *ysp*. Dion translated the word *mqṭr* as "incense altar" based on similar words in Akkadian (*maqtaru*, among others) and South Arabian texts.

A third ritual context known as WT-13 was located approximately 20 km east of 'Ataruz and 4 km southwest of Mudayna Wadi al-Thamad (Figure 21) (Daviau 2017a; Dolan 2007). Unlike 'Ataruz and Mudayna Wadi al-Thamad, the ritual context was located outside of, but adjacent to, a settlement 300 m to the south of Rujm al-Rumayil, a small ninth- through seventh-century fortified settlement that exhibited a circular design with a stone tower in its center and a dry moat marking its perimeter.[56] Rujm al-Rumayil and WT-13 were located on a north–south road,

---

[56] A survey of the area surrounding al-Rumayil and WT-13 identified caves, cisterns, and sherd scatters, an indication that the landscape surrounding these sites was anything but empty (Foley in Daviau 2017a: 247–272).

leading Daviau to interpret WT-13 as a wayside shrine for travelers (e.g., Horvat Qitmit (Beit-Arieh 1995)). WT-13 was founded in the tenth century; evidence recovered from the earliest phases suggests that feasting was a common activity (Stratum III; Daviau 2017a: 22–39). The structure was abandoned during the ninth century, and after a hiatus of a century, the shrine was reconstituted during the eighth and seventh centuries, this time with a rectilinear temenos perimeter wall preserved three stone courses high that created an interior space of ~85 m^2 accessed through a narrow door (AA) in the northeast corner (Stratum IIC-A; Daviau 2017a: 39–75; fig. 3.26). An L-shaped stone bench (A1:20–21) about 1.75 m in length was built just inside the threshold; additional partition walls and possible benches were built sporadically throughout the room. Ceramic bowls, kraters, and cooking pots (Daviau 2017a: 52–59; figs. 3.22–31) and ritual equipment were also found throughout the room in a series of laminated surfaces. These objects were more densely concentrated on the western side, suggesting this area was the focus of ritual activity. Ritual equipment was also identified near short stone walls, likely benches for ritual activity, abutting the main walls (Daviau 2017a: 69). The profile of the recovered faunal evidence indicates that meals consisting of sheep and goat were prepared in the building (Lipovitch in Daviau 2017a: 204–212). However, these animals were not butchered in the building, nor were large cuts of meat consumed there, an indication that stages of the feasting ritual took place outside of the building. The building passed out of use in the late seventh or early sixth century, possibly abandoned during the nearby destruction of Mudayna Wadi al-Thamad.

An ancient visitor to WT-13 would have encountered hundreds of images of miniature humanoid figures and possibly deities surrounded by a menagerie of votive objects inside the building. These objects included polished stone beads, pendents, shells, rare stones in unusual shapes, and weaving equipment (Daviau 2017a: 137–170). Some of these objects were not local to the region and may have been thought of as "exotic" by those who deposited them in the room. Ceramic altars, model shrines, and cult stands were likely numerous, as small broken fragments found in the building attest (e.g., Daviau 2017a: 142–152; figs. 5.3-.5). An assemblage of at least twenty-one anthropomorphic ceramic statues were also located in the building, most of them discovered in fragmentary condition (Figure 22) (Daviau 2017: 108–128). These statues were hollow, legless but free-standing figures ranging in height between 10 and 50 cm, with some fragments suggesting much larger statues once existed.[57] Facial features, hair, headgear, and breasts were shaped in ceramic. Statues' hands were either

---

[57] Parallels for these statues are present at other Iron Age wayside shrines in the Negev, such as Horvat Qitmit (Beit-Arieh 1995: 43–45).

Figure 22 Humanoid ceramic figure found inside the shrine at WT-13 (Reworked after Daviau 2017a: fig. 4.8).

separated or clasped, and resting on the figure's abdomen, or holding their breasts or objects, presumedly offerings. Pigments on the statues' bodies indicate that they were polychromatic and may have represented clothing. In one instance, a lamp was attached to the statue's head (Daviau 2017a: 112–113; fig. 4.8). All of these characteristics together suggest that they more likely represent worshippers than deities. Yet by far the most abundant object type ($n = 91$) in WT-13 were small (<15 cm tall) handmade and mold-made ceramic relief figurines depicting humans in a forward-facing direction holding objects such as discs or clasping their breasts (Daviau 2017a: 81–108). Based on displayed sexual characteristics, a significant majority of the figurines present as females. The extent to which these figurines represent worshippers or deities is a matter of debate.[58]

There have been multiple noble attempts to synthesize the evidence described in this section into something resembling "Moabite religion," that

---

[58] Concerning the growing field of research on ceramic figurines from west-central Jordan, see, most recently, Daviau and Zeran 2021; and Hunziker-Rodewald 2021 for the most recent contributions.

is, a systematic description of what first-millennium BCE societies "believed" and how they materialized these beliefs through ritual practice. Indeed, this topic has by far been the most popular theme in the study of Moab during the past two decades. Yet the evidence defies attempts to achieve this goal. Mesha's rhetoric accords with the biblical writers who convey the cult of Kemosh was widely practiced across the region. There is no reason to doubt that Kemosh was a prominent deity who was worshipped in temples and shrines across west-central Jordan. There is textual evidence suggesting the worship of other deities was popular at points in the region's history. Were Moab's kings so successful in promoting Kemosh's cult that the worship of these legacy deities were extinguished? Unfortunately, the archaeological evidence for ritual practice reviewed here, which is notably robust and well documented, cannot yet contribute an answer to this question. What the archaeological evidence indicates, however, is that ritual practice followed multiple pathways in west-central Jordan, from sacrifices in kingdom-sponsored public temples at settlements such as Dhiban and Karak to smaller shrines nestled in dense settlements at 'Ataruz and Mudayna Wadi al-Thamad to wayside shrines and familial residences.

7 Responding to Assyrian Imperialism

The kingdom of Moab faced a new international power beginning in the late eighth century when the kingdom of Assyria expanded its political and economic reach into the southern Levant from its traditional homeland in what is today northern Iraq (Bagg 2017; Frahm 2017). Moab was not immune to the Assyrian empire's imperial ambitions (Vera Chamaza 2005). Evidence for the exact date in which the kingdom became an Assyrian vassal is lacking, although the event likely took place around 734 BCE during Tiglath-Pileser III's fifth campaign to the Levant, a venture in which the Assyrian army reached Egypt's border. Multiple southern Levantine kingdoms, including Moab's neighbors to the north and south, Ammon and Edom, respectively, became Assyrian vassals during this campaign. A tribute list found in the archives of Nimrud's Fort Shalmaneser dating from the same year mentions Moab, although the tablet is too fragmentary to determine what the kingdom offered the empire.[59] A later royal inscription from c. 728 BCE listed a Salāmānu of Moab among the Levantine kings who paid Tiglath-Pileser tribute of luxury goods and precious metals.[60] What goes unmentioned is that this Salāmānu likely swore a loyalty

---

[59] See CDLI P224664 at http://oracc.org/atae/P224664/.
[60] See line r 10' of Q003460 (K 3751) at http://oracc.org/rinap/Q003460/.

oath to the Assyrian king in which he pledged to send regular amounts of tribute to his new patron in exchange for his protection. This practice of tribute payments and gift giving continued over the next several decades. A letter from Sargon II's reign reports that emissaries from Moab and its neighbor delivered forty-five horses to the royal court,[61] while Kammūsunadbi is said to have delivered extensive gifts and kissed the feet of Sennacherib, the Assyrian king, around 703/702 BCE.[62] Muṣurī is listed among many kings from whom Esarhaddon requested buildings materials for his new palace at Nineveh in 673 BCE;[63] the same king offered gifts to Ashurbanipal, Esarhaddon's successor.[64] These regular tribute payments and gift-bearing visits to the royal court gained Moab a limited degree of political and economic autonomy while sparing itself from the violent destruction that less compliant kingdoms (e.g., Arpad, Aram-Damascus) in the northern Levant experienced. Only once is Moab described as acting disloyal toward the empire in 713 BCE in one of Sargon's royal inscriptions accusing Moab and its neighbors of paying tribute to the Egyptians.[65]

Aside from the occasional mention of Moab's kings and their ability to remain in Assyria's good graces, the sources reveal little about how Assyrian control impacted the communities of west-central Jordan. Earlier scholars assumed that Assyria directly administered Moab and its neighbors as provinces despite the cuneiform sources that suggest local kings maintained their autonomy so long as their loyalty toward Assyria was sustained. In an often-cited early statement, for instance, Oded extrapolated a series of assumptions from Assyrian records describing how the empire ruled adjacent Levantine territories to argue that similar conditions likely existed in western Jordan (Oded 1970). Yet, as Bennett (Bennett 1982: 187) and later Bienkowski (Bienkowski 2000) argued, the invasive imperial rule that Oded and others envisioned does not accord with the archaeological evidence. Indeed, recent investigations of Assyrian records, particularly the correspondence between kings and provincial officials, have determined that the empire used a range of strategies to administer the empire's periphery (Aster and Faust 2018; McGinnis et al. 2016; Parker 2001; Tyson and Herrmann 2018). Any correspondence of this nature is unfortunately lacking for west-central Jordan,

---

[61] For ND 02765, see r7 at http://oracc.org/saao/P224487/.
[62] See line 37 at http://oracc.org/rinap/Q003478/.
[63] See line v56 at http://oracc.org/rinap/Q003230/.
[64] See line ii 29' at http://oracc.org/rinap/Q003705/. An undated letter found at Nineveh describes a gift of gold from a ruler of Moab. See line 4 at http://oracc.org/saao/P334437/.
[65] See line vii 27" in http://oracc.org/rinap/Q006563.

leaving only the archaeological evidence to measure how the region's communities responded to Assyrian imperialism.

One sign that west-central Jordan's inhabitants escaped the Assyrian military's wrath is the lack of evidence for the violent destruction of settlements in the second half of the eighth century. Instead, as has already been described, key settlements that were prominent in the ninth and eighth centuries such as ʻAtaruz, Dhiban, and Madaba show evidence of abatement during the seventh century. This decline seen at select settlements should not be mistaken for an overall decline in west-central Jordan, however. At Baluʻa, the settlement's population grew in size during the seventh century, expanding beyond the eastern fortification walls already described. Residences excavated in this new neighborhood contained ceramic vessels dating to the seventh century, including distinct carinated bowls often assumed to be imports from Assyria (Areas CI, CIII; Worschech 1995: figs. 2–3). Settlements such as Hisban, al-Mashhad, and al-Mukhayyat also continued into the seventh century, finally declining later in that century or the following sixth century, reasons for which will be discussed soon.

Ongoing research at Baluʻa will soon make a major contribution to this question of Assyria's impact on the region as will the final publications of Mudayna Wadi al-Thamad, ancient Yaḥas, a settlement 140 m long and 80 m wide and surrounded by a sloping glacis c. 20 m wide (Figure 23) (Chadwick 2018; Chadwick et al. 2024; Daviau 1997). The settlement was founded a few centuries earlier, as was already described, although how early remains debated. The final settlement, which spans the seventh century, was destroyed in the early sixth century, likely during a Babylonian campaign. The settlement was entered through a six-chambered gate on the north side of the settlement. A domestic area (Complex 300) was located on the settlement's west side consisting of multiple rectangular buildings constructed adjacent to one another (Daviau et al. 2008: 345–350; Daviau et al. 2012: 281–288; fig. 26). Evidence for food production and storage was abundant in specific rooms. An industrial zone dedicated to textile weaving and dying was located on the settlement's east side (Complex 200). At the settlement's south end, Complex 400 consisted of multiple adjacent rectangular rooms (Daviau and Klassen 2014: fig. 2A; Daviau et al. 2008: 350–354). The large number of recovered objects, including objects imported from outside the region, suggest the building's owners fled in haste just prior to the settlement's destruction in the sixth century.[66]

---

[66] Consult Chadwick et al. 2024 for updated building plans and interpretations.

Figure 23 Khirbat Mudayna on the Wadi al-Thamad, looking east, with excavation fields labeled (Khirbat al-Mudayna eth-Thamad ©APAAME_20191029_RHB-0053. Photograph: R. Bewley).

Settlements like Baluʻa and Mudayna Wadi al-Thamad may have benefitted from the favorable economic conditions that took hold in the seventh century following an earlier century of upheaval brought on by Assyrian aggression. Signals of economic intensification in select craft and agricultural industries are visible in the archaeological evidence, such as an increase in olive oil production on the southern Levantine coastal plain (Gitin 1997) and the crafting of carved ivories and metal platters in Phoenicia and western Syria (Feldman 2014). Some scholars attribute these noticeable changes to Assyria's deliberate attempts to stimulate the Levant's economies for their own benefits (Gitin 1995; Younger 2015), while others interpret changes as responses by local agents who increased production in order to participate in new international markets connecting the Mediterranean Sea and Mesopotamia (Faust 2018; Schloen 2001: 146–147). Similar signs of economic intensification during the seventh century are admittedly difficult to identify in west-central Jordan. Given the demand on Moab to deliver annual payments of tribute to Assyria in order to remain in the empire's good standing, the kingdom's administration was likely somewhat concerned about their constituents' abilities to produce enough surplus that could be extracted to support these payments. Grain agriculture production and animal husbandry may have expanded into the eastern edge of the Karak Plateau, where soil quality and precipitation were barely sufficient for agricultural production. Multiple farmsteads, usually consisting of a building and a tower, have been surveyed in these zones and found to date to the seventh and sixth centuries (Porter et al. 2014: 144–146; Routledge 2004: 192–201; fig. 9.4). Producers may have appreciated the positive economic conditions and relatively low investment risks when carrying out this expansion into less arable lands in hopes of increasing their agricultural yields.

An intensification in animal husbandry would have also produced more animal hair that could be used in the production of textiles.[67] Significant amounts of textile production equipment have been identified at Mudayna Wadi al-Thamad, particularly in Complex 200, a 16 × 23 m complex consisting of three horizontal buildings constructed adjacent to each other (Daviau and Klassen 2014: fig. 8). Wood loom beams, small tools such as spatulas and spindles, and a staggering number of more than 250 loom weights were located alongside twenty-six stone basins, multiple red-stained millstones, and hundreds of pieces of hematite that altogether attest to the fact that textile weaving and dying was the complex's principal focus (Daviau 2017b; Daviau and Klassen 2014: 113–117; figs 8–10; table 2). Daviau interprets this clear evidence for textile production specialization as evidence for economic intensification designed to meet the demands of the Assyrian empire.

One additional economic change was the increased consumption of aromatics starting in the seventh century, usually incense and perfumes that were sourced in south Arabia and then transported northward to markets in the Levant, Mesopotamia, and the Mediterranean. These caravans of precious organic materials passed through west-central Jordan along the King's Highway on their journey to the northern Levant and larger centers such as Damascus. Evidence that communities in the region also used stone altars to consume incense in ritual contexts has already been described. Caravans traveling from Arabia to western Jordan entered the southeast corner of the Karak Plateau to travel up the Fajj al-'Usaiker toward Karak and Balu'a. Guarding the entrance of the Fajj was Mudaybi', a stone-built rectangular complex 7,300 m² with towers fortifying the corners (Mattingly 2015; Pace 2015) (Figure 24). A four-chambered gate was located on one side and was designed with the site's defensive needs in mind. A similar rectangular fort was located at Lahun perched on the edge of the Wadi al-Mujib, likely on or near a road that linked the Karak and Dhiban Plateaus (Homès-Fredericq 1997: 68–78; Homès-Fredericq 2009) (Figure 25).[68] The

---

[67] See Wade and Mattingly 2003 for additional evidence at seventh-century Mudaybi'.
[68] Steiner suggest a seventh-century date for the Lahun fort based on her analysis of the ceramic vessel evidence (Steiner 2014: 774).

Figure 24 Aerial view of Mudaybiʻ looking east. Some first millennium BCE features are obscured by Middle Islamic and Late Islamic architecture (Mudeibi (Miller #435) ©APPAAME_20191024_DS-0327. Photograph: D. Salameen).

Figure 25 Aerial view of Lahun looking north with rectangular fort labeled (Lehun ©APAAME_20170920_MND-0228. Photograph: M. Dalton).

trapezoidal-shaped 43 × 35 m stone complex was built above the southern most corner of the twelfth-century settlement already described. Five towers – four at each corner and a middle tower on the south wall overlooking the Wadi al-Mujib – helped monitor the road and a modest entrance on the complex's north face permitted access.

The seventh-century date of Mudaybi' and Lahun's occupation and their defensive architectural design have led to some speculation that these settlements were strategically placed garrisons where Assyrian soldiers guarded the roads and protected the empire's interests in the region. On the one hand, the presence of Assyrian garrisons in the region would not be surprising, as similar installations have been confidently identified in the southern Coastal Plain, such as Tell Jemmeh and Tell Sera', where distinctive Assyrian architecture and material culture have been recorded (Ben-Shlomo and Van Beek 2014). On the other hand, neither Mudaybi' nor Lahun exhibit architectural features and objects indicative of a direct Assyrian presence. In fact, the evidence that has been presented suggests both settlements are surprisingly lacking in imported objects (Homès-Fredericq 2009; Mattingly 2015). If indeed these settlements were military garrisons monitoring highways, they were staffed with local soldiers and their families, possibly in the employment of the kingdom that had an interest in overseeing long-distance commerce.

This is not to say that imported objects were rare in west-central Jordan during the seventh and early sixth centuries. Mesopotamian (i.e., Assyrian and Babylonian), Egyptian, and Greek objects, many of which can be classified as "luxury" goods, have been found sporadically in settlements and tombs (Bennett 1982; Routledge 1997). For instance, fragments of glazed ceramic bottles were found in the ritual context at WT-13, examined earlier (Daviau 2017a: 194) as well as in a small room (B408) in Complex 400 at Mudayna Wadi al-Thamad (Daviau and Klassen 2014). Petrographic analysis determined that these vessels were manufactured outside of the region, likely in the vicinity of Assur and Nineveh, the Assyrian capitals (Daviau and Klassen 2014: 109). The Mudayna Wadi al-Thamad bottles were associated with other luxury items in the small room, including a small limestone statue, a group of black burnished ceramic vessels, a steatite cosmetic mortar, an alabastron, a calcite pyxis, and multiple faience objects (Daviau and Klassen 2014: 102; fig. 2). Additional Mesopotamian objects were found in nearby buildings at Mudayna Wadi al-Thamad such as distinctive ceramic pointed bottles and storage jars (Daviau and Klassen 2014: figs. 6 and 7).[69] Daviau suggests that the presence

---

[69] These objects may have arrived in west-central Jordan during Assyria's fluorescence in the early to mid-seventh century, remained in circulation after the empire's influence in the region

of these Mesopotamian objects may indicate Assyrians lived at Mudayna Wadi al-Thamad at some point during the seventh century, although it is possible the objects were circulating as prestige goods that were acquired locally, a reflection of how west-central Jordan was linked to the international economies of the seventh century (Routledge 1997).

Based on the current evidence from seventh- and sixth-century west-central Jordan, therefore, Assyrian imperialism was not as invasive as Oded had assumed. Moab's kings appear to have been loyal vassals to Assyria, allowing them to sustain their authority over west-central Jordan, although the details of their administration are unknown. The archaeological evidence indicates that a number of changes took place in the region during the seventh century. Settlement patterns were disrupted with some experiencing decline, while others grew in population; industries such as grain, animal, and textile production intensified; and foreign luxury goods circulated through the region. The fact that these patterns persisted decades after the withdrawal of the Assyrian empire in c. 640 suggests that Moab's economy was durable enough to withstand changes in international politics. Did Moab's kings motivate and sustain these economic conditions out of a need to meet Assyria's tribute requirements and take advantage of new opportunities in regional markets demanding dyed textiles? Or were households and communities seizing the initiative themselves in order to participate in regional and international markets? Just who or what motivated these changes remains a question for further investigation.

8 The End of Moab?

West-central Jordan's textual and archaeological records are fragmentary after the seventh century, making it challenging to determine the status of Moab's political organization in the second half of the first millennium BCE. The Assyrian empire's power over the Levant began to wane c. 640 BCE as the sons of Ashurbanipal began their succession feuds that continued until Nineveh's destruction in 612. In the wake of Assyria's decline, the Egyptian state under the rule of Psamtik I and Necho II, two prominent pharaohs of the 26th Dynasty, expanded its influence over the Levant, particularly the port cities of the Mediterranean littoral (e.g., Ashkelon, Tyre). The extent to which Egypt's influence extended east of the Jordan Rift Valley at this time is difficult to determine based on the present

---

declined starting c. 640 BCE, and were eventually deposited in their findspots during the early-sixth century destruction of the settlement.

evidence. Nor is it possible to determine how Assyria's waning influence may have affected Moab's kings.

The Babylonian Empire's rise in the very late seventh and early sixth centuries likely compromised whatever autonomy Moab's kings had enjoyed under Assyria. Moab seems to have been spared from the empire's early violent campaigns under Nebuchadnezzar, whose armies dismantled many of its neighbors to the west, laying siege to major settlements such as Ashkelon (604 BCE), and deporting populations to southern Mesopotamia. A passing mention of a king of Moab with the patron deity's theophoric, *Kemoš*[–], written on an ostracon at Lachish dated to c. 589 BCE suggests the royal office continued into the sixth century (no. 8; Lemaire in Ussishkin 2004: 2106–2107). If Josephus's account is to be trusted in his *Antiquities* (10.181–2),[70] Nebuchadnezzar campaigned against Moab and its northern neighbor, Ammon, during the twenty-third year of his reign, c. 582 BCE, just a few years after the Lachish ostracon was written.[71] Josephus reports that the Babylonian king successfully made subjects of Moab's residents. Major settlements such as Dhiban were already in decline before the seventh century. The limited amount of evidence for settlement ceases during the late seventh and early sixth centuries BCE. These abatement episodes, however, cannot yet be linked to a specific military campaign or internal economic collapse. The violent destructions that are hallmarks of Assyrian and Babylonian campaign activities in the Levant are difficult to detect in west-central Jordan. The gate and surrounding buildings at Mudayna Wadi al-Thamad may be a rare exception, however (e.g., Field D, Building 306; 315; Daviau et al. 2012: 281–288). A large number of abandoned ceramic vessels, some of which date to the early sixth century, were found on the floors of buildings that were destroyed through burning (Daviau and Klassen 2014: 118). A similar pattern may possibly be seen at Balu'a, where the final settlement episodes in residences have been dated to the late seventh and early sixth centuries BCE (Bramlett, Vincent, and Ninow 2018: 2).[72]

Whatever remained of Moab's political organization by the mid sixth century may have suffered at the hands of Babylon's final king, Nabonidus, whose attacks against Edom in southern Jordan are documented in the Nabonidus Chronicle[73]

---

[70] See the Greek and English translation at www.loebclassics.com/view/josephus-jewish_antiquities/1930/pb_LCL326.259.xml.

[71] In a thoughtful publication, Tyson argues that Josephus's date is incorrect and tentatively suggests a later date under Nabonidus's rule was more likely (2013). It is possible, of course, that the armies of both Babylonian kings campaigned through western Jordan three decades apart.

[72] Excavation is ongoing at Balu'a, so this link between Balu'a's end and the Babylonian's campaign must be accepted cautiously. The investigators write, "The ceramic forms from the final phase of the house date to the Late Iron Age II or even into the Persian period, while retaining mostly late Iron Age II characteristics" (Bramlett, Vincent, and Ninow 2018: 2).

[73] See Nabonidus Chronicle i line 17: "[…] they set up camp [against E]dom." (Grayson 1975: 105; cf. Crowell 2007: 78).

(Grayson 1975: 105) and in an inscription adjacent to an image of the king on a rock relief at Sela' (DaRiva 2020). Crowell convincingly dates this attack against Edom to 551 BCE, Nabonidus's fifth year (Crowell 2007). If correct, Moab may have seen similar violence around this time. That Moabites were deported to Mesopotamia, as were so many other members of Levantine communities, is suggested by the recording of two individuals bearing the theophoric element "Kemosh" in their names, Kamušušarraušu and Kamušuilu, in late sixth-century documents found in southern Mesopotamia dated to the reign of Darius I (c. 522–486 BCE).[74]

With the collapse of the Babylonian Empire in 539 BCE, the Levant fell under the control of the Achaemenid Persian Empire who ruled from its distant capitals in southwest Iran (Jacobs 2021). The Levant was administered as part of the Ebir-Nāri, or the "Beyond the [Euphrates] River," satrap and was sub-divided into provinces controlled by governors, many of whom were appointed by the imperial court. The archaeological and textual evidence for the Ebir-Nāri satrap is significantly limited in some regions, making it impossible to characterize Levantine society in general terms during the fifth and fourth centuries (Kaelin 2021). This is especially true for the whole of western Jordan, a region to which the Achaemenid Empire apparently paid little attention compared to the Mediterranean coastline, where the empire held commercial interests. Western Jordan was likely valued for its role as a geographic buffer between the Mediterranean and the Arab tribes (e.g., the Qedarites) who sought to expand west from their bases in north Arabia (Graf and Hausleiter 2021). Sixth- and fifth-century evidence from settlements, such as al-'Umayri (Stratum 6–5; Herr, Clark, and Bramlett 2009: 90–93) and Busayra (Stage 3; Bienkowski 2002: 476; table 14.1), indicate that sedentary lifestyles continued in western Jordan.

Yet there remains a frustrating paucity of material evidence dating between the sixth and the fourth centuries that one could use to characterize the history and societies of west-central Jordan (Bienkowski 2008). Major settlements (e.g., 'Ataruz, Balu'a, Dhiban, and Lahun) demonstrate a noticeable gap in occupation during these centuries. Archaeological surveys have detected ceramic evidence in very limited amounts across the Madaba Plains, the Dhiban, and the Karak Plateaus. Because there is little knowledge of ceramic vessel assemblages between the sixth and fourth centuries, surveys have assigned a poorly defined category of "Iron IIC / Persian" to a broad range of materials. This lack of temporal resolution makes it

---

[74] Text published in Contenau 1929: no. 193. See Cornell 2016: 6–8 and Zadok 1978: 62 for in-depth characterizations of these two sources. A third late use of the Kemosh theophoric was identified in Aramaic on Papyrus 13 (column C, line 10) at mid-fifth-century Saqqara, *Kemošplṭ* (Aimé-Giron 1931: 62; Bowman 1941: 313). If indeed a Moabite, this individual may have made their way to Egypt alongside other Levantine individuals whose names have been identified in documents from Achaemenid-era Egyptian settlements, the most notable being the Elephantine Island community.

impossible to determine settlement occupation dates from the survey evidence at any satisfactory resolution. Nevertheless, the evidence that has been reported for the sixth through fourth centuries indicates a marked abatement in the number of occupied settlements compared to the earlier ninth through seventh centuries. On the Dhiban Plateau, thirteen sites, or ~3 percent of the investigated sites yielded Persian period ceramics (Ji and Lee 2000: 494; table 1), while on the Karak Plateau, twenty sites out of a total of 443 sites with Iron IIC/Persian ceramics were identified with only one settlement yielding more than five sherds (Miller 1991: 203–205). The evidence from the Madaba Plains was slightly more abundant compared to the southern regions, with sixty-three sites, or 43% of investigated sites, yielding Persian-era ceramics (Ibach 1987: 163–168; table 3.11, 13; fig. 3.6).[75] The evidence indicates that a multi-century abatement in sedentary settlement practices commenced at some point in the sixth century and lasted until the second century BCE. What exactly catalyzed this abatement in sedentary settlement? Did Assyria's decline and Babylonian incursions have such a destabilizing effect on west-central Jordan that made it impossible to sustain Moab's political organization and sedentary lifestyles during the era of Achaemenid rule? To be sure, the textual and archaeological sources together indicate that the region remained populated at some level. Determining how west-central Jordan's societies reorganized themselves between the sixth and second centuries BCE will require more research in the years to come.

The final centuries of the first millennium BCE saw the rise of small kingdoms adjacent to west-central Jordan who took advantage of a power vacuum created by a weakened Seleucid Empire's withdrawal from the southern Levant. To the west was a resurgent Judea ruled by the Hasmonean Dynasty between 140 and 37 BCE (Atkinson 2016; Berlin and Kosmin 2021). The first-century CE historian Flavius Josephus retrospectively reported in his *Antiquities of the Jews* that Alexander Yannai (103–76 BCE) conquered the territories of the "Arabs of Moab" and forced them to pay tribute (*Ant* 13.374, 382).[76] Another passage lists Hisban, Madaba, and other towns in Moab among those controlled by the Hasmoneans (*Ant.* 13.397).[77] To the south of west-central Jordan was the kingdom of Nabataea whose wealth was earned through its transport of incense, spices, and other luxury goods from Arabia to Mesopotamia and the Mediterranean (Graf 2021; Markoe 2003). The historian Diodorus, writing in

---

[75] See also Bienkowski 2008: 339 for a review of the evidence from the Madaba Plains, the Dhiban Plateau, and the Karak Plateau surveys.
[76] See www.loebclassics.com/view/josephus-jewish_antiquities/1930/pb_LCL365.413.xml?rskey=NDJfTQ&result=8.
[77] Visit www.loebclassics.com/view/josephus-jewish_antiquities/1930/pb_LCL365.427.xml?result=8&rskey=NDJfTQ.

312/311 BCE a few decades after the campaigns of Alexander the Great, described the Nabateans as incessantly nomadic aside from their political gatherings at "a certain rock," a monument most likely denoting Petra (Diodorus 19.94–97).[78] Diodorus's description confines the Nabataeans to southern Jordan in the fourth century, leaving open the question of how far north nomadic groups had settled by that point in time. By the late second and early first century BCE, however, Nabataean settlements are visible in the material record of western Jordan, including west-central Jordan (Schmid 2008: 360–366). Archaeological surveys have detected the distinctive "Nabataean" painted ceramic vessels alongside other Hellenistic assemblages throughout west-central Jordan in abundance. On the Karak Plateau, for instance, 290 out of 443 survey sites, or 65%, yielded Nabataean ceramics on their surface (Miller 1991: 209–211). These patterns attest to the widespread presence of sedentary settlements in west-central Jordan, a level of intensity not seen since the seventh century BCE. Nabataean temples have been identified at Dhiban (Tushingham 1972: 34–39; plan 3), Dhat Ras (Eddinger 2004), Khirbat al-Dharih (Villeneuve and al-Muheisen 1988), and Tannur (McKenzie 2013). A Nabataean-era house dated to the first centuries BCE and CE was documented at the base of Mudayna Wadi al-Thamad's Iron Age fortifications (Field N; Daviau et al. 2012: 291–297; fig. 48). If indeed the Nabataeans were a population that had migrated from Arabia to western Jordan, rejuvenating sedentary settlement practices throughout the region, how did indigenous "Moabite" populations receive these new arrivals? These and related questions about the transition between the Iron Age and the Hellenistic Period in west-central Jordan remain to be answered.

When surveying the evidence for the second half of the first millennium BCE, therefore, the textual and archaeological record are ambiguous about exactly when Moab's political organization dissolved. However, the fragmentary sources indicate that the term "Moab" persisted as a geographic signifier for the region and its residents. From the beginning of the first millennium CE onward, the Moab toponym makes cameo appearances in place names in west-central Jordan. The Roman Empire annexed western Jordan in 106 CE, placing the region under the province of Arabia Petraea. Ptolemy lists two major settlements that preserve Moab's names, Rabbathmoba ('Ραβάθμωβα; modern Rabba; *Geography* 5.17.6), and Karakmoba (Χαράκμωβα; Karak; *Geography* 5.17.5) (Stückelberger and Graßhoff 2006: 578–579). Eusebius mentions in his *Onomasticon* several towns, their locations, and characteristics he affiliates with Moab (e.g., ’Αροηρ, 'Aro'er, 12:5; Δειβων, Dhiban, 80:5; among many others). The so-called Madaba Map,

---

[78] Visit www.loebclassics.com/view/diodorus_siculus-library_history/1933/pb_LCL390.87.xml for the Greek text and translation.

a sixth-century CE mosaic map of settlements on either side of the Jordan River and Dead Sea, preserves a small fragment of Karakmoba's name in Greek as [... α] xμωβ[α] (Piccirillo and Alliata 1999). Historians and geographers writing in Arabic, such as the ninth-century al-Ya'qubi (e.g., *Ta'rikh* 1:48) and the tenth-century al-Muqaddasi (*Aḥsan al-Taqasim* 178, 192; al-Muqaddasi 1994),[79] also recognize the name Moab as an antecedent for the more common geographic term, al-Balqa', which grew in popularity toward the end of the first millennium CE and remains a popular geographic term in modern Jordan.

Conclusion

To write "against Moab" is not to disparage the ancient kingdom, as the late eighth-century Judahite prophet Isaiah did in his oracle (15:1–9), nor argue for the futility of its investigation. The intention has been quite the opposite, in fact. This examination of the archaeological and historical record from second- and first-millennia BCE west-central Jordan has determined that the scaffolding of evidence that has been constructed for "Moab" is flimsy, a fact that calls into question what one can say about the ancient kingdom and its constituents with any confidence. This gossamer framework is largely due to the fact that the available evidence resists confident interpretations. The survey coverage of west-central Jordan, for instance, is certainly impressive, and the evidence makes it possible to identify the breadth of first millennium BCE settlements throughout the region. Yet, upon the excavation of key settlements (e.g., Balu'a, Dhiban, Hisban, Karak), archaeologists have discovered that first-millennium settlements were often dismantled by later Classical and Islamic-era building projects, making it difficult-to-impossible to document intact cultural deposits. Where secure first millennium deposits have been identified, their investigation has focused more on questions concerning chronology over those that pertain to contemporary archaeological research, say, about agricultural economies, craft production, and social archaeology. As a result, the published results of these excavations can do little more than describe the design of buildings and their dates of occupation.

Moab notably resists interpretation when scholars insist on prioritizing observations of external commentators. It is understandable why scholars of ancient Israel are drawn to investigate its neighbor Moab, yet they often do so using a lens that gives primacy to the biblical narrative. The consequences of doing so, as has been demonstrated here, often leads to skewed interpretations of the evidence, whether it was Glueck's and van Zyl's early reconstructions of Moab or more recent efforts to locate an early kingdom of Moab in the late second millennium

---

[79] Al-Muqaddasi writes, "Ma'āb lies in the mountains. It has many villages, producing almonds and grapes. It is close to the desert" (178).

BCE among the region's agropastoralist villages (Finkelstein and Lipschits 2011; Luria 2021). The evidence is overinterpreted to "fit" the biblical narrative in such a way that the accuracy and the logic of the biblical source remains irrefutable. That is to say, for these scholars, the biblical description of Moab always must be – and already always was – historically accurate. Egyptian and Assyrian sources offer even less information about Moab. Like the biblical evidence, campaign itineraries and tribute lists cast Moab as a (very) minor and (very) passive character in a narrative in which Egypt and Assyria are the principal protagonists. Egypt and Assyria seemed so unconcerned about Moab that even a passing mention of the kingdom in the historical record is indeed surprising.

It is frustrating to discover, then, that the problems created by these external sources are not easily corrected for by texts so far recovered from west-central Jordan. Indeed, the interpretation of these sources raises just as many questions as they supply answers. Like the archaeological evidence, these texts are fragmentary (e.g., the Karak Inscription) and at times difficult to interpret with confidence (e.g., the 'Ataruz Inscription). Records describing Moab's economic organization are absent as are any literary records – a Moabite "bible," for instance – that could shed light on ritual and religion. Notably, a significant number of seals and seal impressions presumed to be associated with Moab through visual elements and inscriptions lack a known provenance. The MI – the longest Northwest Semitic inscription yet to be discovered – does not offer historical information about events on either side of the ninth century BCE. Compounding these issues further, scholars use historical analogies and social scientific categories to paste over gaps in knowledge and problematic evidence. Audiences then depart with a confident impression of Moab that glosses over the challenges with the primary sources.

The next decade will thankfully see the publication of more evidence from excavation projects at 'Ataruz, Balu'a, Dhiban, Khirbat al-Mukhayyat, Khirbat Safra, Mudaybi', and Mudayna Wadi al-Thamad, among others. As the investigation of Moab unfolds during the next few decades, this new evidence will offer opportunities to strengthen this evidentiary scaffold as well as test the interpretive bonds that hold it together. One significant change scholars can make to enhance the quality of west-central Jordan's archaeological record is to pay greater attention to the ways excavated evidence is documented and sampled. In order to characterize Moab's food economies, for instance, more robust sampling methods and analyses of paleobotanical and faunal evidence are required. Additionally, radiocarbon analysis of short-lived botanical samples from deposits suspected to date before the ninth century, that is, before the onset of the Hallstatt Plateau that obscures dates after that century, is needed. Not only do changes need to be made about what projects excavate and analyse, but also changes regarding where scholars concentrate their work. The southern half of the Karak Plateau, for instance, has seen little investigation, aside from the excavations at Mudaybiʻ, compared to the amount that has been carried out between Madaba and Karak. Archaeological surveys have identified second- and first-millennium settlements in this region, including on the edge of the Wadi al-Hasa (Clark et al. 1994: 45–47). Excavations in this specific region will fill a spatial gap in the field's knowledge. At-risk archaeological sites that are subject to destruction by climate change, modern settlement encroachment, and clandestine looting activities should be identified and prioritized for investigation. Yet, even with these new developments, Moab's fragmentary textual and archaeological record will no doubt continue to resist interpretation, defying scholars' desires to present a complete picture of ancient Israel's neighbor. Arriving at the point where Moab can be appreciated on its own terms, rather than through the quips of biblical prophets and Israel's epic tales, is the challenge that lies ahead.

References

Ababsa, M. (2014). *Atlas of Jordan's History, Territories, and Society*. Beirut: Presses de l'IFPO.

Aimé-Giron, N. (1931). *Textes araméens d'Égypte*. Cairo: L'Institut Français d'Archéologie Orientale.

Albertz, R., & Schmitt, R. (2012). *Family and Household Religion in Ancient Israel and the Levant*. Winona Lake: Eisenbrauns.

al-Muqaddasi, M. (1994). *The Best Divisions for Knowledge of the Regions: A Translation of Ahsan al-Taqasim fi Ma'rifat al-Aqalim*. (B. Collins, Trans.). Reading, UK: Centre for Muslim Contribution to Civilization.

Aster, S. Z., & Faust, A., eds. (2018). *The Southern Levant under Assyrian Domination*. University Park: Eisenbrauns.

Atkinson, K. (2016). *A History of the Hasmonean State: Josephus and Beyond*. London: Bloomsbury.

Avigad, N., & Sass, B. (1997). *Corpus of West Semitic Stamp Seals*. Jerusalem: Israel Exploration Society.

Bagg, A. M. (2017). Assyria and the West. In E. Frahm, ed., *A Companion to Assyria*. Chichester: Wiley, pp. 268–274.

Barrick, W. B. (1991). The *bamoth* of Moab. *MAARAV: A Journal for the Study of the Northwest Semitic Languages and Literatures*, 7: 67–89.

Bean, A. L., Rollston, C. A., McCarter, P. K., & Wimmer, S. J. (2018). An inscribed altar from the Khirbat Ataruz Moabite sanctuary. *Levant*, 50: 211–236.

Beit-Arieh, I., ed. (1995). *Horvat Qitmit: An Edomite Shrine in the Biblical Negev*. Tel Aviv: Institute of Archaeology, Tel Aviv University.

Bell, G. (1908). *Syria: The Desert and the Sown*. London: W. Heinemann.

Ben-David, C. (2001). The 'Ascent of Luhith' and the 'Road to Horonaim': New Evidence for their Identification. *Palestine Exploration Quarterly*, 133: 136–144.

Bender, F. (1974). *Geology of Jordan*. Berlin: Gebruder Borntraeger.

Benedettucci, F. (2022). *Tell al-Mashhad: Lo Scavo*. Monte Compatri: Edizioni Espera.

Bennett, C. M. (1982). Neo-Assyrian influence in Transjordan. In A. Hadidi, ed., *Studies in the History and Archaeology of Jordan I*. Amman: Department of Antiquities, pp. 181–187.

Ben-Shlomo, D., & Van Beek, G. W., eds. (2014). *The Smithsonian Institution Excavation at Tell Jemmeh, Israel, 1970–1990*. Washington, DC: Smithsonian Institution Scholarly Press.

Benz, F. L. (1972). *Personal Names in the Phoenician and Punic Inscriptions*. Rome: Biblical Institute Press.

Berlin, A. M., & Kosmin, P. J. (2021). *The Middle Maccabees: Archaeology, History, and the Rise of the Hasmonean Kingdom*. Atlanta: Society for Biblical Literature.

Bienkowski, P. (2000). Transjordan and Assyria. In L. E. Stager, J. A. Greene, & M. D. Coogan, eds., *The Archaeology of Jordan and Beyond: Essays in Honor of James A. Sauer*. Winona Lake: Eisenbrauns, pp. 44–58.

Bienkowski, P. (2002). *Busayra: Excavations by Crystal-M. Bennett 1971-1980*. Oxford: Oxford University Press

Bienkowski, P. (2008). The Persian Period. In R. Adams, ed., *Jordan: An Archaeological Reader*. Sheffield: Equinox, pp. 335–352.

Bowman, R. A. (1941). An Aramaic journal page. *The American Journal of Semitic Languages and Literatures*, 58: 302–313.

Bramlett, K., Vincent, M., & Ninow, F. (2017). Baluʻa 2017. *Newsletter of the Institute of Archaeology, Siegfried H. Horn Museum*, 39(1): 1–3.

Bramlett, K., Vincent, M. D., & Ninow, F. (2018). Khirbat al-Baluʻa. In *Archaeology in Jordan Newsletter: 2016 and 2017 Seasons*. Amman: American Center of Oriental Research, pp. 61–62.

Bright, J. (1959). *A History of Israel*. Philadelphia: Westminster Press.

Chadwick, R. (2018). The 2012 season at Khirbat al-Mudayna ath-Thamad: Exterior gate rooms and a cave tomb. In *Studies in the History and Archaeology of Jordan XII*. Amman: Department of Antiquities, pp. 301–316.

Chadwick, R., Daviau, P. M. M., Steiner, M., & Judd, M. (2024). *The Iron Age Town of Mudayna Thamad, Jordan*. Oxford: British Archaeological Reports

Clark, D., Herr, L., LaBianca, Ø., & Younker, R., eds. (2015). *The Madaba Plains Project: Forty Years of Archaeological Research into Jordan's Past*. Sheffield: Equinox.

Clark, G., Olszewski, D. I., Schuldenrein, J., Rida, N., & Eighmey, J. D. (1994). Survey and excavation in Wadi al-Hasa: A preliminary report of the 1993 field season. *Annual of the Antiquities of the Department of Jordan*, 38: 41–56.

Clark, V. A., Cocky, F. L., & Parker, S. T. (2006). The Regional Survey. In S. T. Parker, ed., *The Roman Frontier in Central Jordan: Final Report on the Limes Arabicus Project, 1980–1989*. Washington, DC: Dumbarton Oaks.

Cline, E. H. (2014). *1177 B.C.: The Year Civilization Collapsed*. Princeton: Princeton University Press.

Contenau, G. (1929). Textes Cunéiformes 13. *Contrats Néo-Babyloniens*. Paris: Musée du Louvre.

Cordova, C. (2007). *Millennial Landscape Change in Jordan: Geoarchaeology and Cultural Ecology*. Tucson: University of Arizona.

Cornell, C. (2016). What happened to Kemosh? *Zeitschrift für die alttestamentliche wissenschaft*, 128: 284–299.

Crowell, B. L. (2007). Nabonidus, as-Silaʿ, and the beginning of the end of Edom. *Bulletin of the American Schools of Oriental Research*, 348: 75–88.

Crowfoot, J. W. (1934). An expedition to Baluʿah. *Palestine Exploration Fund*, 66: 76–84.

Da Riva, R. (2020). The Nabonidus inscription in Sela (Jordan): Epigraphic study and historical meaning. *Zeitschrift für Assyriologie und Vorderasiatische Archäologie*, 110(2): 176–195.

Danielson, A., & Foran, D. (2021). Iron Age Nebo: Preliminary investigations at Khirbat al-Mukhayyat and Rujm al-Mukhayyat, Jordan. *Palestine Exploration Quarterly*, 153: 83–112.

Danielson, A. J., Foran, D., Klassen, S., Braun, G., Ginson, G., & Doležálková, V. (2024). Life on the Margins: The Early Iron Age Site of ʿAyun adh-Dhib, Jordan. *Levant*, 1–12.

Darnell, J. C., & Jasnow, R. (1993). On the Moabite inscriptions of Ramesses II at Luxor Temple. *Journal of Near Eastern Studies*, 52(4): 263–274.

Daviau, P. M. M. (1997). Moab's northern border: Khirbat al-Mudayna on the Wadi ath-Thamad. *Biblical Archaeologist*, 60(4): 222–228.

Daviau, P. M. M. (2017a). *A Wayside Shrine in Northern Moab: Excavations in the Wadi ath-Thamad*. Oxford: Oxbow Books.

Daviau, P. M. M. (2017b). Industrial furnishings at Khirbat al-Mudayna ath-Thamad: Clues from Egyptian Culture. In M. Neeley, G. Clark, & P. M. M. Daviau, eds., *Walking through Jordan: Essays in Honor of Burton MacDonald*. Sheffield: Equinox, pp. 39–62.

Daviau, P. M. M., Chadwick, R., Weigl, M., et al. (2012). Excavation at Khirbat al-Mudayna and survey in the Wadi ath-Thamad: Preliminary report on the 2008, 2010, and 2011 seasons. *Annual of the Department of Antiquities of Jordan*, 56: 269–308.

Daviau, P. M. M., Dolan, A., Ferguson, J., et al. (2008). Preliminary report of excavations and survey at Khirbat al-Mudayna ath-Thamad and in its surroundings (2004, 2006 and 2007). *Annual of the Department of Antiquities of Jordan*, 52: 343–374.

Daviau, P. M. M., & Klassen, S. (2014). Conspicuous consumption and tribute: Assyrian glazed ceramic bottles at Khirbat al-Mudayna ath-Thamad. *Bulletin of the American Schools of Oriental Research*, 372: 99–122.

Daviau, P. M. M., & Steiner, M. L. (2000). A Moabite sanctuary at Khirbat al-Mudayna. *Bulletin of the American Schools of Oriental Research*, 320: 1–21.

Daviau, P. M. M., & Zeran, E. (2021). Astarte on her horse at Khirbat al-Mudayna in Northern Moab. In E. D. Darby and I. J. de Hustler, eds., *Iron Age Terracotta Figurines from the Southern Levant in Context*. Leiden: Brill, pp. 256–284.

Dearman, A., ed. (1989). *Studies in the Mesha Inscription and Moab*. Atlanta: Scholars Press.

Dion, P. E., & Daviau, P. M. M. (2000). An inscribed incense altar of Iron Age II at Ḥirbet el-Mudēyine (Jordan). *Zeitschrift des Deutschen Palästina-Vereins*, 116: 1–13.

Dolan, A. E. (2007). *Wadi ath-Thamad Site WT-13: A Hermeneutical Approach to Moabite Religion*. Dissertation, University of Toronto.

Dolan, A. E., & Edwards, S. J. (2020). Preference for periphery? Cultural interchange and trade routes along the boundaries of late Iron Age Moab. *Palestine Exploration Quarterly*, 152: 53–72.

Drinkard, J. F. (1989). The literary genre of the Mesha inscription. In A. Dearman, ed., *Studies in the Mesha Inscription and Moab*. Atlanta: Scholars Press, pp. 131–154.

Drinkard, J. F. (1997). New volute capital discovered. *The Biblical Archaeologist*, 60: 249–250.

Eddinger, T. W. (2004). A Nabatean/Roman temple at Dhat Ras, Jordan. *Near Eastern Archaeology*, 67: 14–25.

Edwards, S. (2019). Omride architecture at the town of Nebo. *Zeitschrift des Deutschen Palästina-Vereins*, 135: 143–157.

Eggler, J., Keel, O., & Ben-Tor, D. (2006). *Corpus der Siegel-Amulette aus Jordanien: Vom Neolithikum bis zur Perserzeit*. Fribourg: Academic Press.

Elkins, S. P. (2019). *Ceramic Architectural Models from the Madaba Plains Region: A Selected Art Historical Analysis*. PhD Dissertation, LaSierra University.

El-Naqa, A. (1993). Hydrological and hydrogeological characteristics of Wadi el-Mujib catchment area, Jordan. *Environmental Geology (Berlin)*, 22(3): 257–271.

Farahani, A., Miller, M. J., Porter, B. W., Dawson, T., & Routledge, B. (2023). Stable isotopes of archaeological and modern semi-terrestrial crabs (*Potamon potamios*) provide paleoecological insights into brachyuran ecology and human resource acquisition in late Holocene Jordan. *Quaternary International*, 658: 14–23.

Farahani, A., Porter, B. W., Huynh, H., & Routledge, B. (2016). Crop storage and animal husbandry at Early Iron Age Khirbat al-Mudayna al-'Aliya (Jordan): A paleoethnobotanical approach. In K. McGeough, ed., *The Archaeology of Agro-Pastoralist Economies in Jordan*. Boston: American Schools of Oriental Research, pp. 27–89.

Faust, A. (2018). The Southern Levant under the Neo-Assyrian Empire: A comparative perspective. In C. W. Tyson & V. R. Herrmann eds., *Imperial Peripheries in the Neo-Assyrian Period*. Louisville, Colorado: University Press of Colorado.

Faust, A., & Bunimovitz, S. (2003). The four room house: Embodying Iron Age Israelite society. *Near Eastern Archaeology*, 66(1–2): 22–31.

Feldman, M. (2014). *Communities of Style: Portable Luxury Arts, Identity, and Collective Memory in the Iron Age Levant*. Chicago: University of Chicago.

Finkelstein, I. (2013). *The Forgotten Kingdom: The Archaeology and History of Northern Israel*. Atlanta: Society of Biblical Literature.

Finkelstein, I., & Lipschits, O. (2011). The genesis of Moab: A proposal. *Levant*, 43(2): 139–152.

Finkelstein, I., Na'aman, N., & Römer, T. (2019). Restoring line 31 in the Mesha Stele: The "House of David" or Biblical Balak. *Tel Aviv*, 46: 3–11.

Foran, D., Harrison, T., Graham, A., Barlow, C., & Johnson, N. (2004). The Tall Madaba archaeological project, preliminary report of the 2002 field season. *Annual of the Department of Antiquities of Jordan*, 48: 79–96.

Frahm, E., ed. (2017). *A Companion to Assyria*. Hoboken: Wiley.

Frevel, C. (2023). *History of Ancient Israel*. Atlanta: Society for Biblical Literature.

Fried, L. S. (2002). The high places (*bāmôt*) and the reforms of Hezekiah and Josiah: An archaeological investigation. *Journal of the American Oriental Society*, 122: 437–465.

Fried, M. (1967). *The Evolution of Political Society: An Essay in Political Anthropology*. New York: Random House.

Gitin, S. (1997). The Neo-Assyrian Empire and its western periphery: The Levant, with a focus on Philistine Ekron. In S. Parpola & R. M. Whiting, eds., *Assyria 1995*. Helsinki: Neo-Assyrian Text Corpus Project, pp. 77–103.

Gilboa, A. (2014). The Southern Levant (Cisjordan) during the Iron Age I period. In A. E. Killebrew & M. Steiner, eds., *Oxford Handbook of the Archaeology of the Levant*. Oxford: Oxford University Press, pp. 624–648.

Glueck, N. (1934). *Explorations in Eastern Palestine I*. New Haven: American Schools of Oriental Research.

Glueck, N. (1939). *Explorations in Eastern Palestine III*. New Haven: American Schools of Oriental Research.

Glueck, N. (1940). *The Other Side of the Jordan*. New Haven: American Schools of Oriental Research.

Graf, D. F. (2021). The Nabataeans. In T. Kaizer, ed., *A Companion to the Hellenistic and Roman Near East*. Hoboken: John Wiley & Sons, pp. 272–283.

Graf, D. F., & Hausleiter, A. (2021). The Arabian world. In B. Jacobs & Rollinger, R., eds., *A Companion to the Achaemenid Persian Empire*. Hoboken: Wiley & Sons, pp. 529–551.

Graham, M. P. (1989). The discovery and reconstruction of the Mesha inscription. In A. Dearman, ed., *Studies in the Mesha Inscription and Moab*. Atlanta: Scholars Press, pp. 41–92.

Grayson, A. K. (1975). *Assyrian and Babylonian Chronicles*. Locust Valley: J.J. Augustin.

Gregor, P. (2021). Preliminary report on the Khirbat as-Safra survey 2017. *Annual of the Department of Antiquities of Jordan*, 60: 531–537.

Gregor, P., Ray, P., Gane, C., Broy, T., & Moody, J. (2021). Preliminary report on the 2018 season of excavations at Khirbat aṣ-Ṣafrā. *Annual of the Department of Antiquities of Jordan*, 60: 539–547.

Harrison, T. P. (1997). Intrasite spatial analysis and the settlement history of Madaba. In G. Bisheh, ed., *Studies in the History and Archaeology of Jordan VI*. Amman: Department of Antiquities, pp. 137–142.

Harrison, T. P. (2009). "The land of Medeba" and Early Iron Age Madaba. In P. Bienkowski, ed., *Studies on Iron Age Moab and Neighbouring Areas in Honour of Michèle Daviau*. Leuven: Peeters, pp. 27–45.

Harrison, T. P., & Barlow, C. (2005). Mesha, the *mishor*, and the chronology of Iron Age Madaba. In T. Levy & T. Higham, eds., *The Bible and Radiocarbon Dating: Archaeology, Text and Science*. London: Equinox, pp. 179–190.

Herr, L. G., Clark, D. R., & Bramlett, K. (2009). From the Stone Age to the Middle Ages in Jordan: Digging up Tall al-'Umayri. *Near Eastern Archaeology*, 72: 68–97.

Homès-Fredericq, D. (1997). *Decouvrez Lehun et la Voie Royale / en de Koningsweg*. Comite Belge de Fouilles en Jordanie / Belgische Comite voor Opgravingen in Jordanie.

Homès-Fredericq, D. (2009). The Iron Age II fortress of al-Lahun (Moab). In P. Bienkowski, ed., *Studies on Iron Age Moab and Neighbouring Areas in Honour of Michèle Daviau*. Leuven: Peeters, pp. 165–182.

Hogue, T. (2022). For god, king and country: Cult and territoriality in the Iron Age Levant. *Levant*, 54(3), 347–358.

Hunziker-Rodewald, R. (2021). Molds and mold-links: A close view on the female terracotta figurines from Iron Age II Transjordan. In E. Darby & I. de Hulster, eds., *Iron Age Terracotta Figurines from the Southern Levant in Context*. Leiden: Brill, pp. 220–255.

Hunziker-Rodewald, R., & Deutsch, R. (2014). The Shihan stele reconsidered. *Transeuphratène*, 45: 51–67.

Ibach, R. D. (1987). *Hesban 5: Archaeological Survey of the Hesban Region*. Berrien Springs: Institute of Archaeology, Andrews University.

Issar, A. S., & Zohar, M. (2004). *Climate Change: Environment and Civilization in the Middle East*. Berlin: Springer.

Jackson, K. P. (1989). The language of the Mesha inscription. In A. Dearman, ed., *Studies in the Mesha Inscription and Moab*. Boston: American Schools of Oriental Research, pp. 96–130.

Jacobs, B., & Rollinger, R. (2021). *A Companion to the Achaemenid Persian Empire*. Chichester: Wiley Blackwell.

Jacobs, L. (1983). Survey on the south ridge of Wadi 'Isal, 1981. *Annual of the Department of Antiquities of Jordan*, 27: 245–274.

Jang, D. (2009). An integrative study of the Moabite religion during the Iron Age II period: Glimpsing religion in text and context. *The Mediterranean Review*, 1(2): 39–62.

Ji, C. H. (2007). The 'Iraq al-Amir and Dhiban Plateau Regional surveys. In T. Levy, P. M. Daviau, R. Younker, & M. Shaer, eds., *Crossing Jordan: North American Contributions to the Archaeology of Jordan*. London: Equinox, pp. 137–142.

Ji, C. H. (2011). Khirbat 'Ataruz: An interim overview of the 10 years of archaeological architectural findings. *Annual of the Department of Antiquities of Jordan*, 55: 561–579.

Ji, C. H. (2012). The Early Iron Age II temple at Hirbet 'Atarus and its architecture and selected cultic objects. In J. Kamlah, ed., *Temple Building and Temple Cult: Architecture and Cultic Paraphernalia of Temples in the Levant (2.-1. Mill. B.C.E.)*. Wiesbaden: Harrassowitz Verlag, pp. 203–221.

Ji, C. H. (2016). One tale, two 'Ataruz: Investigating Rujm 'Ataruz and its association with Khirbat 'Ataruz. *Studies in History and Archaeology of Jordan*, 12: 211–222.

Ji, C. H. (2018). A Moabite sanctuary at Khirbat Ataruz, Jordan: Stratigraphy, findings, and archaeological implications. *Levant*, 50: 173–210.

Ji, C. H., & Bates, R. D. (2017). Khirbat 'Ataruz 2011–12: A preliminary report. *Annual of the Department of Antiquities of Jordan*, 58: 303–327.

Ji, C. H., & Lee, J. K. (1998). Preliminary report of the survey on the Dhiban Plateau, 1997. *Annual of the Department of Antiquities of Jordan*, 42: 549–571.

Ji, C. H., & Lee, J. K. (2000). A preliminary report on the Dhiban Plateau survey project, 1999: The Versacare expedition. *Annual of the Department of Antiquities of Jordan*, 44: 493–506.

Kaelin, O. (2021). The Levant. In B. Jacobs & R. Rollinger, eds., *A Companion to the Achaemenid Persian Empire*. Chichester: Wiley Blackwell, pp. 583–593.

Kitchen, K. A. (1992). The Egyptian evidence on ancient Jordan. In P. Bienkowski, ed., *Early Edom and Moab: The Beginning of the Iron Age in Southern Jordan*. Sheffield: J.R. Collis, pp. 21–34.

Klassen, S., & Danielson, A. (2023). Copper trade networks from the Arabah: Re-assessing the impact on Early Iron Age Moab. In E. Ben-Yosef, & I. Jones, eds., *"And in Length of Days Understanding" (Job 12:12): Essays on Archaeology in the Eastern Mediterranean and Beyond in Honor of Thomas E. Levy*. Cham: Springer, pp. 1201–1226.

Kyle, M. G. (1908). Some geographic and ethnic lists of Rameses II at the Temple of Luxor. *Recueil de Travaux relatifs à la Philologie et à l'Archéologie égyptiennes et assyriens*, 30: 222–223.

LaBianca, Ø. (1990). *Hesban 1: Sedentarization and Nomadization*. Berrien Springs: Andrews University Press.

LaBianca, Ø., & Younker, R. W. (1995). The kingdoms of Ammon, Moab, and Edom: The archaeology of society in Late Bronze/Iron Age Transjordan (ca. 1400–500 BCE). In T. E. Levy, ed., *The Archaeology of Society in the Holy Land*. New York: Facts on File, pp. 399–415.

Langgut, D., Finkelstein, I., & Litt, T. (2013). Climate and the Late Bronze collapse: New evidence from the Southern Levant. *Tel Aviv*, 40(2): 149–175.

Lemaire, A. (1994). "House of David" restored in Moabite inscription. *Biblical Archaeological Review*, 20(3): 30–37.

Lemaire, A. (2021). La stèle de Mésha: Problèmes, épigraphiques, philologiques et chronologiques. In H. Niehr, & T. Römer, eds., *Nouvelles Recherches autour de la Stèle de Mésha / Neue Forschungen zur Méscha-Stele*. Wiesbader: Harrassowitz, pp. 141–174.

Lev-Tov, J., Porter, B., & Routledge, B. (2011). Measuring local diversity in early Iron Age animal economies: A view from Khirbat al-Mudayna al-'Aliya (Jordan). *Bulletin of the American Schools of Oriental Research*, 361: 67–93.

Levy, T. E., Najjar, M., & Ben-Yosef, E. (2014). *New Insights into the Iron Age Archaeology of Edom, Southern Jordan: Surveys, Excavations and Research from the University of California, San Diego – Department of Antiquities of Jordan Edom Lowlands Regional Archaeology Project (ELRAP)*. Los Angeles: Cotsen Institute of Archaeology Press.

Lipschits, O. (2011). The origin and date of the volute capitals from the Levant. In I. Finkelstein & N. Naʻaman, eds., *The Fire Signals of Lachish: Studies in the Archaeology and History of Israel in the Late Bronze Age, Iron Age, and Persian Period in Honor of David Ussishkin*. Winona Lake: Eisenbrauns, pp. 203–225.

Luria, D. (2021). Why were Moab's gigantic Iron I fortifications necessary? A new research approach. *Revue Biblique*, *128*(3): 390–403.

MacDonald, B. (2000). *"East of the Jordan:" Territories and Sites of the Hebrew Scriptures*. Boston: American Schools of Oriental Research.

MacGinnis, J., Wicke, D., & Greenfield, T., eds. (2016). *The Provincial Archaeology of the Assyrian Empire*. Cambridge: McDonald Institute for Archaeological Research.

Macumber, P. G. (2008). Evolving landscape and environment in Jordan. In R. Adams, ed., *The Archaeology of Jordan*. Sheffield: Sheffield Academic Press, pp. 7–34.

Markoe, G. (2003). *Petra Rediscovered: Lost City of the Nabataeans*. Cincinnati: Cincinnati Art Museum.

Mattingly, G. L. (1989). Moabite religion. In A. Dearman, ed., *Studies in the Mesha Inscription and Moab*. Boston: American Schools of Oriental Research, pp. 213–238.

Mattingly, G. L. (2015). Long-distance trade on the Karak Plateau (Central Jordan): The case of Khirbat al-Mudaybiʻ and Fajj al-ʻUsaykir. *Review & Expositor*, 112(2): 288–300.

McKenzie, J. (2013). *The Nabataean Temple at Khirbet et-Tannur, Jordan: Final Report on Nelson Glueck's 1937 Excavation*. Boston: American Schools of Oriental Research.

Milgrom, J. (1990). *Numbers*. Philadelphia: Jewish Publication Society.

Milik, J. T. (1958–1959). Nouvelles inscriptions Sémitiques et Grecques du Pays de Moab. *Liber Annuus*, 9: 330–358.

Miller, J. M., ed. (1991). *Archaeological Survey of the Kerak Plateau*. Atlanta: Scholars Press.

Miller, J. M. (1992). Early monarchy in Moab? In P. Bienkowski, ed., *Early Edom and Moab: The Beginning of the Iron Age in Southern Jordan*. Sheffield: J.R. Collis Press, pp. 77–91.

Mittmann, S. (1981). The ascent of Luhith. In A. Hadidi, ed., *Studies in the History and Archaeology of Jordan I*. Amman: Department of Antiquities, pp. 175–180.

Morton, W. H. (1989). The 1954, 55, and 65 excavations at Dhiban in Jordan. In A. Dearman, ed., *Studies in the Mesha Inscription and Moab*. Atlanta: Scholars Press, pp. 239–246.

Mumford, G. D. (2013). Egypt and the Levant. In M. Steiner & A. E. Killebrew, eds., *The Oxford Handbook of the Archaeology of the Levant: c. 8000–332 BCE*. Oxford: Oxford University Press, pp. 69–89.

Murphy, R. E., & Carm, O. (1952). A fragment of an Early Moabite inscription from Dibon. *Bulletin of the American Schools of Oriental Research*, 125: 20–23.

Na'aman, N. (2019). The alleged "Beth David" in the Mesha Stele: The case against it. *Tel Aviv*, 46: 192–197.

Niehr, H., & Römer, T., eds. (2021). *Nouvelles recherches autour de la Stèle de Mésha = Neue Forschungen zur Mescha-Stele: Kolloquium des Collège de France, des Musée du Louvre und des Deutschen Vereins zur Erforschung Palästinas anlässlich der 150*. Wiesbaden: Harrassowitz Verlag.

Oded, B. (1970). Observations on methods of Assyrian rule in Transjordan after the Palestinian campaign of Tiglath-Pileser III. *Journal of Near Eastern Studies*, 29: 177–186.

Olavarri, E. (1965). Sondage a Aro'er sur l'Arnon. *Revue Biblique*, 72: 77–94.

Olavarri, E. (1969). Fouilles a 'Aro'er sur l'Arnon. *Revue Biblique*, 76: 230–259.

Olavarri, E. (1993). Aroer (in Moab). In E. Stern, A. Lewinson-Gilboa, & J. Aviram, eds., *The New Encyclopedia of Archaeological Excavations in the Holy Land*. Jerusalem: Israel Exploration Society, pp. 92–93.

Pace, J. H. (2015). The origin and purpose of Khirbat al-Mudaybi'. *Review & Expositor*, 112(2): 280–287.

Parker, B. J. (2001). *The Mechanics of Empire: The Northern Frontier of Assyria as a Case Study in Imperial Documents*. Helsinki: The Neo-Assyrian Text Corpus Project.

Parker, S. B. (2002). Ammonite, Edomite, and Moabite. In J. Kaltner & S. L. McKenzie, eds., *Beyond Babel: A Handbook for Biblical Hebrew and Related Languages*. Atlanta: Society of Biblical Literature, pp. 43–60.

Parker, H. D. D., & Arico, A. F. (2015). A Moabite-inscribed statue fragment from Kerak: Egyptian parallels. *Bulletin of the American Schools of Oriental Research*, 373: 105–120.

Parker, S. B. (2002). Ammonite, Edomite, and Moabite. In J. Kaltner & S. L. McKenzie, eds., *Beyond Babel: A Handbook for Biblical Hebrew and Related Languages*. Atlanta: Society of Biblical Literature, pp. 43–60.

Parker, S. T. (2006). *The Roman Frontier in Central Jordan: Final Report on the Limes Arabicus Project, 1980–1989*. Washington, DC: Dumbarton Oaks Research Library and Collection.

Petter, T. (2014). *The Land between the Two Rivers: Early Israelite Identities in Transjordan*. Winona Lake: Eisenbrauns.

Philip, G. (2008). The Early Bronze Age I-III. In R. Adams, ed., *Jordan: An Archaeological Reader*. London: Equinox, pp. 161–226.

Piccirillo, M., & Alliata, E. (1999). *The Madaba Map Centenary, 1897–1997: Travelling through the Byzantine Umayyad Period*. Jerusalem: Studium Biblicum Franciscanum.

Porter, B. W. (2007). *The Archaeology of Community in Iron I Central Jordan*. Dissertation, University of Pennsylvania, Philadelphia.

Porter, B. W. (2013). *Complex Communities: The Archaeology of Early Iron Age West-Central Jordan*. Tucson: The University of Arizona Press.

Porter, B. W. (2014). Toward a socionatural reconstruction of the Early Iron Age settlement system in Jordan's Wadi al-Mujib Canyon. In E. Gubel & I. Swinnen, eds., *From Gilead to Edom: Studies in the Archaeology of Jordan in Honor of Denyse Homès-Fredericq*. Akkadica Supplementum 12, Wetteren: Assyriological Centre Georges Dossin, pp. 133–150.

Porter, B. W., Routledge, B., Fatkin, D., et al. (2010). The Dhiban Excavation and Development Project's 2005 Season. *Annual of the Department of Antiquities of Jordan*, 54: 9–34.

Porter, B. W., Routledge, B., Fatkin, D., et al. (2012). The Dhiban Excavation and Development Project's 2009 Season: Field L Excavations. *Annual of the Department of Antiquities of Jordan*, 56: 111–129.

Porter, B. W., Routledge, B., Simmons, E., & Lev-Tov, J. (2014). Extensification in a Mediterranean semi-arid marginal zone: An archaeological case study from Early Iron Age Jordan's Eastern Karak Plateau. *Journal of Arid Environments*, 104: 132–148.

Porter, B. W., Routledge, B., Steen, D., & al-Kawamlha, F. (2007). The power of place: The Dhiban community through the ages. In T. Levy, P. M. Daviau, R. Younker, & M. Shaer, eds., *Crossing Jordan – North American Contributions to the Archaeology of Jordan*. London: Equinox, pp. 315–322.

Porter, B. W., & Speakman, R. J. (2008). Reading Moabite pigments with laser ablation ICP-MS: A new archaeometric technique for Near Eastern Archaeology. *Near Eastern Archaeology*, 71: 238–242.

Ray, P. J. (2001). *Hesban 6: Tell Hesban and Vicinity in the Iron Age*. Berrien Springs: Andrews University Press.

Ray, P. J. (2003). Kemosh and Moabite religion. *Near East Archaeological Society Bulletin*, 48: 17–31.

Redford, D. (1982). Contact between Egypt and Jordan in the New Kingdom: Some comments on sources. In A. Hadidi, ed., *Studies in the History and*

Archaeology of Jordan I. Amman: Jordanian Department of Antiquities, pp. 115–119.

Reed, W. L., & Winnett, F. V. (1963). A fragment of an Early Moabite inscription from Kerak. *Bulletin of the American Schools of Oriental Research*, 172: 1–9.

Reich, R. (1992). Palaces and residence in the Iron Age. In A. Kempinski, & R. Reich, eds., *The Architecture of Ancient Israel: From the Prehistoric to the Persian Periods*. Jerusalem: Israel Exploration Society, pp. 202–222.

Reisner, G. A., Fisher, C. S., & Lyon, D. G. (1924). *Harvard Excavations at Samaria, 1908–1910*. Cambridge Harvard University Press.

Richard, S. (2014). The Southern Levant (Transjordan) during the Early Bronze Age. In M. Steiner, & A. E. Killebrew, eds., *The Oxford Handbook of the Archaeology of the Levant: c. 8000–332 BCE*. Oxford: Oxford University Press, pp. 330–352.

Richelle, M. (2021). A re-examination of the reading BT DWD ("House of David") on the Mesha Stele. *Eretz Israel*, 34: 152–159.

Roddy, M., Bramlett, K., & Ninow, F. (2024). Khirbet al-Baluʻa. *Archaeology in Jordan*, 4: 2022 and 2023 Seasons, 121–123.

Rosen, A. M. (2007). *Civilizing Climate: Social Responses to Climate Change in the Ancient Near East*. Lanham: Altamira.

Routledge, B. (1997). Mesopotamian "influence" in Iron Age Jordan: Issues of power, identity, and value. *Bulletin of the Canadian Society for Mesopotamian Studies*, 32: 33–41.

Routledge, B. (2000). Seeing through walls: Interpreting Iron Age I architecture at Khirbat al-Mudayna al-ʻAliya. *Bulletin of the American Schools of Oriental Research*, 319: 37–70.

Routledge, B. (2004). *Moab in the Iron Age: Hegemony, Polity, Archaeology*. Philadelphia: University of Pennsylvania Press.

Routledge, B. (2013). On water management in the Mesha inscription and Moab. *Journal of Near Eastern Studies*, 72: 51–64.

Routledge, B. & Halbertsma, D. Forthcoming. Bōz el-Mushelle Revisited: Casemates, Copper and "Early Moab." *Zeitschrift des Deutschen Palastina-Vereins*.

Routledge, B., & Routledge, C. (2009). The Baluʻa Stela revisited. In P. Bienkowski, ed., *Studies on Iron Age Moab and Neighbouring Areas in Honour of Michèle Daviau*. Leuven: Peeters, pp. 71–95.

Routledge, B., Smith, S., Mullan, A., Porter, B., & Klassen, S. (2014). A Late Iron Age I ceramic assemblage from Central Jordan: Integrating form, technology and distribution. In E. van der Steen, J. Boertien, & N. Mulder-

Hymans, eds., *Exploring the Narrative: Jerusalem and Jordan in the Bronze and Iron Ages*. London: Bloomsbury T&T Clark, pp. 82–107.

Sauer, J. A. (1986). Transjordan in the Bronze and Iron Ages: A critique of Glueck's synthesis. *Bulletin of the American Schools of Oriental Research*, 263: 1–26.

Schloen, J. D. (2001). *The House of the Father as Fact and Symbol: Patrimonialism in Ugarit and the Ancient Near East*. Winona Lake: Eisenbrauns.

Schmid, S. (2008). The Hellenistic period and the Nabataeans. In R. Adams, ed., *Jordan: An Archaeological Reader*. London: Equinox, pp. 353–411.

Seetzen, U. J. (1854). *Reisen durch Syrien, Palastina, Phonicien, die Transjordan-Lander, Arabia Petraea und Unter Aegypten*. Berlin: G. Reimer.

Service, E. (1978). Classical and modern theories of the origins of government. In R. Cohen & E. Service, eds., *Origins of the State: The Anthropology of Political Evolution*. Philadelphia: Institute for the Study of Human Issues, pp. 21–34.

Shiloh, Y. (1970). The four-room house: Its situation and function in the Israelite city. *Israel Exploration Journal*, 20: 180–190.

Shiloh, Y. (1979). *The Proto-Aeolic Capital and Israelite Ashlar Masonry*. Qedem 11. Jerusalem: Institute of Archaeology, Hebrew University of Jerusalem.

Snyder, J. (2010). Did Kemosh have a consort (or any other friends)? Re-assessing the Moabite pantheon. *Ugarit-Forschungen*, 42: 645–675.

Stallard, M. S. (2011). *Paradise Lost: The Biblically Annotated Edition*. Macon: Mercer University Press.

Steiner, M. (2013). The Iron Age I pottery of Khirbat al-Lahun. *Annual of the Department of Antiquities of Jordan*, 57: 519–534.

Steiner, M. L. (2014). Moab during the Iron Age II Period. In M. L. Steiner & A. E. Killebrew, eds., *The Oxford Handbook of the Archaeology of the Levant (8000 - 332 BCE)*. Oxford: Oxford University Press, pp. 770–781.

Stordalen, T. (2015). Heshbon – The history of a biblical memory. In R. I. Thelle, T. Stordalen, & M. E. J. Richardson, eds., *New Perspectives on Old Testament Prophecy and History: Essays in Honour of Hans M. Barstads*. Leiden: Brill, pp. 246–263.

Stückelberger, A., & Grasshoff, G. (2006). *Klaudios Ptolemaios Handbuch der Geographie: griechisch-deutsch*. Basel: Schwabe Verlag.

Swinnen, I. M. (2009). The Iron Age I settlement and its residential houses at al-Lahun in Moab, Jordan. *Bulletin of the American Schools of Oriental Research*, 354: 29–53.

Tigay, J. H. (1986). *You Shall Have No Other Gods: Israelite Religion in the Light of Hebrew Inscriptions*. Atlanta: Scholars Press.

Timm, S. (1989). *Moab Zwischen den Mächten: Studien zu Historischen Denkmèalern und Texten*. Wiesbaden: Harrassowitz.

Tufnell, O. (1953). The Shihan warrior. *Iraq*, 15(2): 161–166.

Tushingham, A. D. (1972). *The Excavations at Dibon (Dhiban) in Moab: The Third Campaign 1952–1953*. New Haven: American Schools of Oriental Research.

Tushingham, A. D. (1990). Dhiban reconsidered: King Mesha and his works. *Annual of the Department of Antiquities of Jordan*, 49: 182–192.

Tushingham, A. D., & Pedrette, P. (1995). Mesha's citadel complex (Qarḥoh) at Dhiban. *Studies in the History and Archaeology of Jordan*, 5: 151–159.

Tyson, C. W. (2013). Josephus, Antiquities 10.180–82, Jeremiah, and Nebuchadnezzar. *Journal of Hebrew Scriptures*, 13: 1–16.

Tyson, C. W., & Herrmann, V. R., eds. (2018). *Imperial Peripheries in the Neo-Assyrian Period*. Louisville: University Press of Colorado.

Tyson, C. W., & Ninow, F. (2019). A basalt volute capital fragment from el-Baluʻ, Jordan. *Zeitschrift des Deutschen Palästina-Vereins*, 135: 158–167.

Ussishkin, D., ed. (2004). *The Renewed Archaeological Excavations at Lachish (1973–1994)*. Tel-Aviv: Insitute of Archaeology, Tel Aviv University.

van Zyl, A. H. (1960). *The Moabites*. Leiden: E.J. Brill.

Vera Chamaza, G. W. (2005). *Die Rolle Moabs in der neuassyrischen Expansionspolitik*. Munster: Ugarit Verlag.

Villeneuve, F., & al-Muheisen, Z. (1988). Fouilles à Khirbet edh-Dharih (Jordanie), 1984–1987 – un village, son sanctuaire et sa nécropole aux époques nabatéenne et romaine (Ie – IVe siècles ap. J.-C.). *Comptes rendus des séances de l'année – Académie des inscriptions et belles-lettres*, 132(2): 458–479.

Wade, J. M., & Mattingly, G. L. (2003). Ancient weavers at Iron Age Mudaybiʻ. *Near Eastern Archaeology*, 66: 73–75.

Ward, W. A., & Martin, M. (1964). The Baluʻa stele: A new transcription with paleographic and historical notes. *Annual of the Department of Antiquities of Jordan*, 8–9: 5–35.

Weber, M. (2017). Two(?) lion reliefs from Iron Age Moab: Further evidence for an architectural and intellectual koiné in the Levant. *Bulletin of the American Schools of Oriental Research*, 377: 85–106.

Weinberg, S. S. (1978). A Moabite shrine group. *Muse*, 12: 30–48.

Winnett, F. V., & Reed, W. L. (1964). *The Excavations at Dibon (Dhiban) in Moab: The First and Second Campaigns*. Baltimore: J.H. Furst.

Worschech, U. (1985). *Northwest Ard el-Kerak 1983 and 1984: A Preliminary Report*. Munich: Manfred Gorg.

Worschech, U. (1995). City planning and architecture at the Iron Age city of al-Baluʻ in Central Transjordan. In K. Amr, F. Zayadine, & M. Zaghloul, eds., *Studies in the History and Archaeology of Jordan V*. Amman: Department of Antiquities, pp. 145–150.

Worschech, U. (2003). *A Burial Cave at Umm Dimis North of el-Baluʻ*. Frankfort: Peter Lang.

Worschech, U. (2014). *Ceramics from el-Balu*. Beiträge zur Erforschung der antiken Moabitis (Ard el-Kerak) 7. Frankfurt: Peter Lang.

Younger, K. L. (2015). The Assyrian economic impact on the Southern Levant in light of recent study. *Israel Exploration Journal*, 65: 179–204.

Zadok, R. (1978). Phoenicians, Philistines, and Moabites in Mesopotamia. *Bulletin of the American Schools of Oriental Research*, 230: 57–65.

Zadok, R. (2020). On a recently found Moabite inscription. *Zeitschrift für die alttestamentliche wissenschaft*, 132: 469–470.

Acknowledgments

A Getty Villa Residential Fellowship in Summer 2022 and a Doreen B. Townsend Center for the Humanities Fellowship in 2023 partially supported research and writing. Thanks to Aaron Burke and Jeremy Smoak, the Cambridge Elements editors, for the invitation, to Andrew Danielson for his assistance with difficult-to-locate publications, and to Robert Bewley and the Aerial Photographic Archive for Archaeology in the Middle East for fulfilling last-minute orders for aerial images. Ron Hendel and two anonymous reviewers offered thoughtful comments on a near-final draft. Thank you to the director and staff of Jordan's Department of Antiquities. This publication was made possible in part by support from the Berkeley Research Impact Initiative (BRII) sponsored by the UC Berkeley Library.

For Stephen C. Jacobs, M.D. (1945–2015)
A scientist with an unmatched love for the humanities

Cambridge Elements=

The Archaeology of Ancient Israel

Series Editors

Aaron A. Burke
University of California, Los Angeles

Aaron A. Burke is Professor of the Archaeology of Ancient Israel and the Levant, and the Kershaw Chair of the Ancient Eastern Mediterranean Studies in the Department of Near Eastern Languages and Cultures at the University of California, Los Angeles, and member of the Cotsen Institute of Archaeology. His research and teaching interests center on the social history of the Levant and Eastern Mediterranean during the Bronze and Iron Ages at the intersections of the study of archaeology, iconography, and texts, including the Hebrew Bible. He has conducted excavations in Jaffa and Tel Dan in Israel.

Jeremy D. Smoak
University of California, Los Angeles

Jeremy D. Smoak is Senior Lecturer in the Department of Near Eastern Languages and Cultures at the University of California, Los Angeles, where he teaches on Hebrew Bible, the history of ancient Israel, and Semitic languages. He is the author of *The Priestly Blessing in Inscription and Scripture: The Early History of Numbers 6:24–26* (Oxford University Press, 2016). He has also published a variety of articles in journals related to archaeology and biblical studies. He has participated in several excavations in Israel and traveled extensively throughout the eastern Mediterranean.

Editorial Advisory Board

Angelika Berlejung, *Leipzig University*
Andrew J. Danielson, *Harvard University*
Marian Feldman, *The John Hopkins University*
Jonathan S. Greer, *Grand Valley State University*
Rachel Hallote, *Purchase College*
Ido Koch, *Tel Aviv University*
Lauren Monroe, *Cornell University*
Stefan Münger, *University of Bern*
Benjamin Porter, *The University of California, Berkeley*
J. David Schloen, *The University of Chicago*
Juan Manuel Tebes, *Pontificia Universidad Católica Argentina*
Naama Yahalom-Mack, *Hebrew University*

About the Series

The archaeology of ancient Israel is among the oldest historical archaeologies in practice. Multi-disciplinary approaches that integrate improved readings of biblical texts, new recovery techniques, pioneering scientific analyses, and advances in identity studies have dramatically changed the questions asked and the findings that follow. Elements in the Archaeology of Ancient Israel embodies these developments, providing readers with the most up-to-date assessments of a wide range of related subjects.

Cambridge Elements

The Archaeology of Ancient Israel

Elements in the Series

Edom in Judah: Trade, Migration, and Kinship in the Late Iron Age Southern Levant
Andrew J. Danielson

Against Moab: Interrogating the Archaeology of Iron Age Jordan
Benjamin W. Porter

A full series listing is available at: www.cambridge.org/EAAI

For EU product safety concerns, contact us at Calle de José Abascal, 56–1°,
28003 Madrid, Spain or eugpsr@cambridge.org.

www.ingramcontent.com/pod-product-compliance
Lightning Source LLC
LaVergne TN
LVHW020349260326
834688LV00045B/1624